The Polished Professional

A quick and handy guide for any
manager or business owner

Written by Elizabeth Haas Fountain

CAREER PRESS
180 Fifth Avenue
P.O. Box 34
Hawthorne, NJ 07507
1-800-CAREER-1
201-427-0229 (outside U.S.)
FAX: 201-427-2037

THE POLISHED PROFESSIONAL
A QUICK AND HANDY GUIDE FOR ANY MANAGER OR BUSINESS OWNER
ISBN 1-56414-146-2, $8.95
Cover design by Digital Perspectives
Printed in the U.S.A. by Book-mart Press

To order this title by mail, please include price as noted above, $2.50 handling per order, and $1.00 for each book ordered. Send to: Career Press, Inc., 180 Fifth Ave., P.O. Box 34, Hawthorne, NJ 07507

Or call toll-free 1-800-CAREER-1 (Canada: 201-427-0229) to order using VISA or MasterCard, or for further information on books from Career Press.

Library of Congress Cataloging-in-Publication Data

The polished professional : a quick and handy guide for any manager or business
   owner.
      p.   cm.   -- (Business desk reference)
   Includes index.
   ISBN 1-56414-146-2 $8.95
   1. Business etiquette.   I. Career Press Inc.   II. Series.
HF5389.P65   1994
395'.52--dc20   94-27209
                                                               CIP

The Polished Professional — *How to Put Your Best Foot Forward*

Table of Contents

Introduction v

1 The Order of Precedence 1

2 Greetings and Farewells 9

3 Introductions 15

4 Conversation 33

5 Telephone Etiquette 43

6 Meetings and Appointments 53

7 Nonverbal Communication 61

8 Written Correspondence 81

9 A Potpourri of Etiquette for Business Situations ...103

10 The Most Common Etiquette Mistakes 111

Index 115

Introduction

Behavior is an integral part of creating impressions.
When people are rude, vulgar or unpleasant, they
repulse others and leave a negative impression. On
the other hand, when a person is kind and treats
others with dignity and respect, people will have a
positive impression.

Saying "please" and "thank you" are common
courtesies as are greeting people pleasantly,
maintaining good eye contact during conversation and
not interrupting when someone else is speaking.
People who practice these courtesies are considered
polite. They draw others to them because they are a
pleasure to be around and make people in their
company feel good.

Etiquette is an extension of politeness and courtesy. It
is the code of prescribed rules of behavior for a
specific situation at a given time. People who practice

truly good etiquette are far from snobbish and do not show off their skills.

Etiquette is not a rigid set of rules that never change. The rules must be flexible in order to accommodate the changes that occur within a society. For example, 35 years ago, if a single woman invited a man to dinner at her home, it would have been considered inappropriate; now it is perfectly acceptable.

Today, a married woman has the choice of taking her husband's name or retaining her maiden name. In these times, both ways are socially acceptable.

Now, more than at any other time in civilization, our society is experiencing drastic changes. The traditional family unit shares the spotlight with single-parent homes and people of the same sex living as a family unit. In business, men and women are choosing careers traditionally held by the opposite sex. Further, due to globalization, there is more association with other cultures. Unfortunately, improper behaviors often ruin relationships before they even get a chance to develop. Consequently, the subject of etiquette is relevant today because the rules have been rewritten.

Most of the world was colonized by European countries; therefore, European or continental manners prevail. American business people have found these manners to be conducive to conducting business abroad or at home with foreign associates. This is not to say that no matter where you go everyone does things in the same way. Each culture has its own customs and traditions. If you anticipate doing business with someone from a different country, it is highly recommended that you familiarize yourself with the specific culture and its customs before your initial contact. Being aware can save you and your organization unnecessary embarrassment and may protect your business interests.

This book will acquaint you with current business etiquette. Becoming adept at proper business etiquette is similar to becoming proficient at a sport. The more you practice, the better you become; the appropriate responses will become second nature. Knowing what to do and when to do it will make you shine in many situations, consequently increasing your self-confidence and heightening your level of sophistication.

Before reading further, take the following etiquette quiz. It will help you assess your current knowledge of what is appropriate behavior in various business and social situations.

Remember:

The goal of good etiquette is to bring out the best in the people you encounter and make them feel comfortable in your presence.

What Is Your "EQ" (Etiquette Quotient)?

The following quiz is based on situations that we all face and that often create havoc. Answer the questions and you will have a better understanding of some of the issues that are covered in this book.

WARNING: This quiz is tricky!

1. When replying to business correspondence signed "Mary Doe," who you know is married, how would you address the envelope?

    _____

2. You are at a business/social function where there are several very important people with whom you would like to get acquainted. When would it be appropriate to offer your business card to them?
    a.   As soon as introductions have been made.
    b.   While introductions are being made.
    c.   Just before you bid farewell.
    d.   None of the above.

3. You are the guest at someone's home or office. Should you rise when someone else enters the room?
    a.   Only if you are a man and the guest is a woman.
    b.   Only if the individual is older than you, regardless of sex.
    c.   Only if the individual is a person with disabilities or a woman who is considerably older than you.
    d.   Yes.

4. How would you make introductions between one of your less important clients, Mr. Brown, and your boss, Mary Doe?

    _____
    _____

5. When you see a vaguely familiar face at a cocktail party, what should you do?
    a.   Act as if you have never met before.
    b.   Say hello and pretend that you know the individual's name.
    c.   Walk up to the person and ask, "Have we ever met before?"
    d.   Introduce yourself.

6. You have just been introduced to Mr. Brown. His name tag reads John Brown. How would you address him?

    _____

7. You and your significant other are hosting a dinner party in a restaurant. Included are two other people: your most valued client and his wife. You instruct the waiter to:
    a. Serve in the manner that is most convenient for him.
    b. Serve your client's wife first.
    c. Serve you and your significant other last.

8. How do you greet a visitor in your office?
    a. Say nothing and let the visitor sit where he/she wishes.
    b. Show him/her where to sit.
    c. Be casual and say, "Make yourself at home."

9. You are at a company holiday party. The president of your company and his wife approach you. They are considerably older than you, but both of them know you by name. Whom do you greet first?
    a. The president.
    b. The wife.
    c. The wife, but only if she initiates the handshaking ritual.

10. You are invited to dinner at a fellow associate's home for the first time. Should you take a gift?
    a. Yes, because it is your first visit.
    b. No, because it would be considered too showy.
    c. Yes, because it is appropriate to take a small gift when invited to someone's home.

11. You have received an invitation that is marked R.S.V.P. You are tentatively scheduled to leave town that weekend. What should you do?

    _____

    _____

12. You are a female marketing executive and you have invited your client, Judy Smith, to lunch. Who should immediately follow the host to the table at which you will be seated?
    a. The client, because she is a woman.
    b. You.
    c. Both of you should reach the table simultaneously because you are both women.

13. You are standing with a group of three people who have never met each other, yet you know everyone present. You have forgotten one person's name. What should you do?
    a. Ask the person his/her name so that you can make an introduction.
    b. Wait and hope that someone will sense that you have forgotten a name and will initiate self-introductions.
    c. Leave the encounter when no one is looking.

14. You are dining in a restaurant with the upper management of your company. You and one other person have been served French onion soup. Should you start eating?
    a. Yes, because French onion soup is more difficult to eat when it cools.
    b. No.
    c. No, not until the other person starts eating.

15. You are in the same situation as described above. The only difference is that you are the most senior person. Would it be appropriate for you to start eating your soup?
           Yes _____   No _____

Answers to "EQ" Test

1. Ms. Mary Doe.
2. d.
3. d.
4. "Mr. Brown, may I introduce Mary Doe?"
5. d.
6. Mr. Brown.
7. b and c.
8. b.
9. c.
10. c.
11. Call or write the host/hostess and explain the situation. Find out the latest date when you can reply.
12. b.
13. a.
14. b. Wait until all have been served.
15. No.

The intention of the quiz is not to test your etiquette knowledge, but rather to mentally prepare you for the information contained in this book. Some of the answers may have surprised you; they will be more thoroughly explained later.

1

THE ORDER
OF PRECEDENCE

Many rules of etiquette are based on the *order of precedence*; therefore, it is necessary to devote some time to the three areas where precedence exists and the way the orders of precedence differ.

The order of precedence is the order in which people are:

- addressed
- greeted
- introduced
- referred
- seated
- served

It also determines who has the right of way.

Every organization and institution, private or governmental, has some form of hierarchical structure that defines the order of authority and where responsibility lies — an order of precedence.

It is very important to know the order of precedence within your work group. It is easier to navigate within an organization when you recognize the hierarchy and can demonstrate the appropriate respect for those in authority. This book is mainly concerned with business situations. However, it is important to devote some time also to discussing precedence in diplomatic and social situations because these areas often overlap. For instance, you may find yourself and your significant other mingling at a ground-breaking ceremony where the governor of your state or some other dignitary is in attendance.

Dealing with Dignitaries

The term "dignitary" designates those who are members of the diplomatic corps. The diplomatic corps consists of:

- Elected officials (chiefs of state, police chiefs, mayors, senators, etc.)
- Appointed officials (ambassadors, judges, members of a cabinet, etc.)
- Royalty (kings, queens, dukes, earls, etc.)
- Church officials (bishops, priests, pastors, etc.)
- Officers in the military, when appearing in an official capacity (generals, majors, captains, etc.)

In the true sense of the word, *protocol* is the set of rules that govern etiquette in official life or in ceremonies involving governments and their representatives. One of the most important rules in protocol is the observance of rank and file or precedence.

Precedence was established by the nations represented at the Congress of Vienna in 1815. They based the orders of rank and file on the date and hour when the envoy holding a diplomatic title presented his letters of credentials as opposed to the size or influence of the nation he represented. These rules still apply today unless they are changed by the head of a government. The head of a government or nation may change the order of precedence within his own jurisdiction. This often happens when a country experiences a *coup d'etat* or when new heads of government are empowered.

Within the international diplomatic arena, protocol is extremely important and, when not followed precisely, has been known to jeopardize relationships between nations.

For the purposes of this book, it is important to note that:

- United States government officials have precedence over state officials.
- State officials have a higher ranking than county and city officials.

- Husbands or wives immediately follow their title-holding spouses. (The exception to this rule would be if the spouse is also a member of the diplomatic corps; then he or she would fall into his or her own designated spot.)

The State Department, the governor's office and libraries are excellent sources for this type of information.

Social Situations

"Ladies first." In today's world, this expression is causing many people great confusion. Men complain that they are in a Catch-22 situation when trying to decide whether or not to show traditional deference toward women. Women, on the other hand, say that "chivalry is dead" or that some men still live in the Dark Ages. So what is appropriate in social situations that involve a mixture of men and women with different expectations?

In both formal and informal social situations, the basic rules are:

1. Women have precedence over men.
2. Older people have precedence over younger people as long as they are of the same sex.
3. Smaller groups usually have precedence over larger groups.

There are exceptions to these rules. The first occurs when you know that a particular woman objects to being treated with traditional deference socially. In this case, respect her wishes and adjust your behavior accordingly. When in doubt, be traditional and show deference to women.

> ### *Etiquette Essential:*
>
> ### *Attend to the needs of the group comprised of the fewest people (or the most important person) first.*

The rule pertaining to precedence and group size requires further explanation and is best understood through an example.

You are hosting a party at your home. It is human nature to form into groups. Therefore, you may find some people mingling with one another, some in "groups," and then some "wall-flowers." As the host, you should attend to the needs of the group with the fewest people, in this case the "wall-flowers," before taking care of the larger groups.

In more formal situations, where there is a guest of honor or a distinguished guest, this rule may change. First, attend to the needs of the group that includes the guest of honor or most distinguished guest. Consider the members' rank within each group rather than the size of the group.

The Ladies vs. Women Debate

Another point of confusion involves how to refer to members of the female gender. Women are "ladies" *socially* and when they are addressed collectively. For instance, at a party, you would refer to the "ladies" who are attending; if you were giving a speech, the proper address is still, "ladies and gentlemen." However, some speakers prefer to remain gender neutral and will start their presentations with a greeting similar to "Good day to all of you," which is also acceptable.

In *business*, the appropriate reference is "women." Most women resent being called ladies, girls or gals in the workplace.

Business Situations

Determining precedence is particularly confusing in the workplace. The organizational chart lists people according to their levels of authority. The president or chief executive officer of the company will be listed at the top, and the lowest echelon will be listed at the bottom.

Just as the organizational chart indicates, senior executives have precedence over junior executives. If you have two executives who are on the same level, show deference to the person with the most seniority. If the seniority is approximately the same but there is a wide age differential, show deference to the older person.

As in social situations, after attending to the needs of the groups that consist of the most important people, turn to the smaller groups before addressing the needs of the larger ones.

Clients and/or customers have precedence over fellow associates, regardless of rank. Many people have difficulty with this rule, particularly if the people in question are from different socioeconomic backgrounds.

Consider a situation where the chief executive officer of a utility company meets a homeowner. This customer's business may have little impact on the company's overall sales; however, collectively, individual customers make a significant contribution to the profitability of the company. Therefore, the CEO should show appropriate respect for the customer.

It is appropriate to show deference to associates from competing companies. The best salespeople never criticize their competition. On the contrary, they will speak highly of their biggest competitors. After all, it is easy to compare your product and/or service to a mediocre one. However, comparing your product and/or service to a reputable one can make yours look even better!

At first, order of precedence may seem very confusing. But with time and practice, you will become proficient.

2

GREETINGS AND FAREWELLS

When you are having a bad day, a friendly "hello" can completely turn your mood around. By the same token, when you enter an office and the people don't acknowledge your presence or, worse yet, grumble when you greet them, your mood continues to sour. Polite people greet others sincerely and take the time to bid them farewell. These are examples of common courtesy. However, several rules must be addressed regarding greetings and farewells in the world of business.

Shaking Hands

According to legend, the handshaking ritual originated as a security measure. In medieval times, when two people shook hands, it was a sign of sincerity and meant that neither had "anything up their sleeves." When one extended a hand, the sleeve was pulled up to expose any hidden objects.

In business situations, regardless of gender or position, the appropriate form of greeting and farewell is the handshake. No one should have to initiate the handshaking ritual. It should be a simultaneous gesture for males and females. However, when dealing with older women, you may want to allow them to initiate the handshaking ritual. Many older people bring their traditional social graces to business situations. The same is true with women who are dealing with older men; be aware that they may wait for you to extend your hand to them.

Etiquette Essential:

Always stand when shaking hands.

Both men and women should always stand when shaking hands, regardless of whom they are greeting or bidding farewell. There is an exception to this rule.

When *seated* at a formal dinner function, do not stand up and greet your fellow diners as they approach the table. Simply shake hands and greet the people sitting to your immediate left and right. If you have never met your dinner companions, shake hands while introducing yourself to them. Be certain to acknowledge the other people sitting at the table. A pleasant greeting and an introduction, if need be, with a nod of the head will suffice. Shake hands with them again when all of you depart from the table.

Should people across the table extend their hands to you, it is recommended that you say something like, "Allow me to make it easier for you," as you walk around the table towards them. *It is very important that you shake hands without any obstacles between you and the other party.* Obstacles could be furniture, counters or people. When you want to shake someone's hand as you are leaving a group, be sure to walk behind the other people to shake hands, as opposed to reaching across the group.

Etiquette Essential:

Always shake hands with your right hand.

The right hand is always used to shake hands. If you need to cough or sneeze, cover your mouth using your left hand.

When attending functions offering opportunities to drink and eat while mingling with the other guests, either eat *or* drink. Do not do both at the same time, unless you have a place to put down your glass or your plate. You should hold the glass or plate in your left hand so that your right hand is free to greet people. Even if you are only enjoying a cocktail, hold the glass in your left hand because the glass is usually cold and may even have condensation. It is unpleasant to shake a cold and wet hand.

On rare occasions, people will extend their left hands to you. This may be due to an injury or disability such as arthritis. When you encounter this, respond with your right hand.

Some people are reluctant to shake hands because they have sweaty palms. If you have this problem, avoid rubbing your hands on your clothes or using tissue prior to shaking someone's hand. Not only does this look bad, but tissue sometimes sticks to a clammy hand, and you may inadvertently pass the tissue to the person with whom you are shaking hands. A better solution is to use antiperspirant on your hand. This should alleviate the problem.

If your hands are cold by nature, shake hands anyway. You may try to warm your hands by wearing gloves if it is appropriate due to weather. However, do not blow on them before shaking hands because it is very unsanitary.

The "glove rule" applies to both men and women. It is appropriate to shake hands while wearing gloves. However, it is better if you remove the glove before you shake hands.

Etiquette Essential:

Never ignore someone who has offered to shake your hand.

To ignore someone's gesture to shake hands is rude. It displays a total lack of consideration for the other person. However, if you find yourself in this awkward situation, simply pull your hand back, smile and politely greet the other person, perhaps by also slightly bowing your head. Remember that some people feel very uncomfortable shaking hands, especially older women who have never worked outside the home. So be aware, because you do not want to make others feel uncomfortable either.

Above all, remember: The goal of good etiquette is to bring out the best in people you encounter and make them feel relaxed and comfortable in your presence. When you make people lose face, you are the one who looks bad.

When you shake hands, you are communicating an impression and are making the other person feel a certain way.

In the United States, handshaking has become a basic formality. However, in many parts of the world, business is still done on a handshake alone. The handshake is a very strong form of nonverbal communication. It says many things about an individual and allows people to "read" others. Remember, handshakes are a physical joining between two people where impressions are created and messages conveyed.

3

INTRODUCTIONS

Making introductions is difficult for some people, yet it is an essential skill in business. If you work for a large company, you are probably called upon to make introductions every day. Some companies are constantly hiring new people, promoting employees and transferring people from department to department.

Regardless of how often you have to make introductions, you need to hone your skills in making formal introductions until it is second nature.

Making introductions is a responsibility. If you are in a situation where you are the only person who knows everyone, it is your responsibility to make the introductions. Think about the alternative. How do you feel when you are with a group of people and you know only one person and that person fails to make introductions? Being the "fifth wheel" is always an uncomfortable position to be in, and a well-mannered person will not allow this to happen to others.

Making good introductions is easy, and after some practice you can do it as smoothly as a White House greeter. A good introduction is short, yet descriptive. This chapter illustrates how important it is to know the order of precedence, because rank plays a very important part in making proper introductions.

Formula for Making Proper Introductions

1. Determine the order of precedence. (Remember, smaller groups have precedence over larger ones.)

2. Say the most distinguished person's first and last names or title and last name, whichever is appropriate.

3. Choose the appropriate introductory statement:
    a. "May I present..." (Most formal, used in the diplomatic corps.)
    b. "May I introduce..." (Recommended for most business and social situations.)
    c. "This is..." (Very casual; it may appear to be unsophisticated.)

4. Say the other people's first and last names or titles and last names, whichever is appropriate. Continue in order of precedence or in the order in which they are standing.

Example

You are responsible for making an introduction between your boss, Mary Brown, and a client, Jerry Byer. You would say: "Jerry Byer, may I introduce Mary Brown."

In the above example, note that Jerry Byer has precedence over Mary Brown because he is the client, regardless of the fact that Mary is a woman.

After the introduction has been made, both parties should know the other person's name and something about that individual. In the previous example, the introduction would have been successful only if both people knew beforehand whom they would be meeting. However, if one of the parties had just joined the encounter, neither would know who the other person was in relation to the introducer. It is helpful to provide some background information about the people you are introducing to one another so they have a place to start conversation. Often, the introducer needs to attend to other matters; providing such information enables him to make a more graceful exit.

Using the previous example, you would say, "Jerry Byer, may I introduce the manager of customer services, Mary Brown. Jerry is our client with the ABC Company." Describe your boss' position or title as opposed to using the term "boss."

Look at what happens when Jerry Byer's wife is included in the example. The order of precedence changes because smaller groups have precedence over larger groups, so you would say Mary Brown's name first. The introduction would be as follows, "Mary Brown, may I introduce Joan and Jerry Byers. Jerry is the buyer from the ABC Company. Mary is our manager of customer services."

The Sophisticated Introducer

Now that you are familiar with the formula for making introductions, it is important to enhance these newly founded skills with a few rules.

1. The sophisticated introducer always stands when making an introduction. The people being introduced should stand as well because, as you have learned in the previous chapter, you should always stand when you are shaking hands.

2. Sometimes, people avoid making introductions because they have forgotten a person's name or have difficulty pronouncing it. The sophisticated introducer admits any problems with an introduction. If you forget someone's name, say something like, "I would like to make an introduction but your name escapes me. Please help me out." Rarely will someone be offended by that. Similarly, if the correct pronunciation is a problem, ask for help. Say, for example, that you want to make an introduction and want to be certain you pronounce the name correctly. Again, most people will appreciate the fact that you are interested enough in them to be accurate.

3. The sophisticated introducer introduces himself when necessary. If you find yourself in a situation where someone has failed to make an introduction, introduce yourself when the appropriate time arises. For instance, when there is a lull in the conversation, you can simply interject, "Hello, I'm Mary Jones," while you extend your hand.

4. The sophisticated introducer appears physically relaxed and poised. Keep your hands out of your pockets while making introductions or when being introduced. This will also help you concentrate on the order of precedence and people's names. Sometimes it is appropriate to gesture toward a person as you say his name. This is especially important in a group so others will know about whom you are speaking.

Etiquette Essential:

It is very important that you introduce people the way they want to be known and addressed.

There are several situations where this rule is particularly important. For instance, it is important when you are introducing a woman with her husband and she has retained her maiden name. You would not introduce them as "Sue Brown and her husband, Barry," because everyone will assume that Barry's last name is Brown. The appropriate introductions would be, "Tom Smith, may I introduce Sue Brown and her husband, Barry Jones."

Another common problem is that you are on a first name basis with someone, yet you know that this person is very formal and prefers to be addressed with a title. Take the situation of a district judge with whom you are on a first name basis. When introducing the judge, do not make the introduction without his appropriate title. You should say, "Judge Smiley, may I introduce my mother, Joanne Black." Because Judge Smiley is an appointed official, he has precedence over your mother, even though she is a woman and may be older than him. If Judge Smiley wishes, he will give permission to your mother to address him by his first name by saying something to the effect, "Please call me Sam, Joanne." However, if he does not, it would be inappropriate for your mother to address him as "Sam."

It is important to listen closely to introductions so you can address people in the way they were introduced. A common mistake is to rely on a name tag. You may be introduced to a Ms. Hall, but if her name tag says Ann Hall, chances are you would call her "Ann." This could be considered brazen or too forward.

Things to Avoid When Making Introductions

The purpose of making introductions is to acquaint people with each other. Introductions need to be short and descriptive with all parties introduced in a complimentary fashion. Often introductions are redundant and too lengthy; the parties are already talking to one another while the introducer is still attempting to make introductions. Many people learned to make introductions by saying "Sue, this is Jim Smith. Jim, this is Sue Brown." Even though this may be considered proper, it is too wordy, and you could find yourself in an awkward situation, especially when making group introductions.

When introducing a group, be efficient. Avoid saying, "Mary Brown, I would like to present..." or "John Brown, I would like to introduce to you..." This is too time-consuming. Avoid using "to you" because it is easy to make the mistake and say "you to." In saying that, you would be reversing the order of precedence. Simply say, "Mary Brown, may I introduce John Smith, the director of operations. Mary is our new marketing manager."

Good introducers always present the parties at their best. If you are making introductions and one of the parties has been recently demoted, there is no need to point that out. However, if the person has been recently promoted, mention that accomplishment.

When business situations become social, introductions need special care to avoid offending anyone. Today, it is commonplace to live with someone and not be married, and it is becoming more prevalent for people of the same sex to live together as a family unit. Even though these people may be very open about their living arrangements, you, as the introducer, need to be careful not to offend other people who may have a different opinion regarding these matters. It is not necessary for the introducer to go into detail about a person's living arrangements or lifestyle; merely introduce each person by name. Leave it up to the parties involved to make their situations known.

However, if you do elect to indicate a relationship between two people who are living together but are not married, it would be appropriate to introduce a partner as the "significant other" or "companion." Couples who share an alternate lifestyle frequently refer to each other as "companions."

Group Introductions

When making group introductions, the introducer's biggest challenge is to keep the attention of everyone present. The introduction needs to be made in the most efficient way possible. This is why the smaller group is mentioned first. Otherwise, you would find yourself repeating names too often.

In most informal situations, when you are a member of a group that is being introduced, suggest self-introductions. Relieving the introducer of his responsibility makes the introductions run more smoothly. After one or more of the people within the group have been introduced, you may initiate self-introductions by stepping in and saying, "Hello, I am Bob Jones, the customer services coordinator." If the introducer did not include positions, avoid giving yours. The rest of the group will surely follow your lead.

Self-introductions are not recommended in formal situations because the parties need to be introduced in the order of precedence. Look at the following situation.

Example

A telephone network salesperson has been asked to give a sales presentation to senior management officials of a company. Prior to this, his only contact with the company has been through the purchasing agent. Upon his arrival, it is the purchasing agent's responsibility to make the introductions. In this particular situation, it is recommended that formal introductions be made in consideration of the salesperson. Most salespeople like to know to whom they are speaking so that they can identify the decision-makers.

In attendance, besides the purchasing agent, are the president, a vice president, the chief financial officer and the systems engineer. The savvy purchasing agent would make introductions in the following manner: "John Bell, may I introduce the president of our company, Jay Head, Larry Hurst, chief financial officer, our vice president of operations, Gary Sweet, and the systems engineer, Mike Murphy. I have been working with John during the past five months..."

You have now learned the formula for making introductions. Remember, you must practice in order to become an adept introducer.

The exercise on the following pages was developed using situations that are common in business. At first, simply practice the formula for making introductions:

1. Determine the order of precedence.
2. Start with the most distinguished person first.
3. Use the introductory statement, "May I introduce..."
4. Say the other person's/people's name(s).

Once you are proficient with the formula, elaborate by adding the background information about the people you are introducing. Remember, keep it "short and sweet."

Introductions Exercise

Situation #1

You are the marketing director for a small company. You have been dealing with a potential client, John Brown, and you would like to turn him over to one of your salespeople, Tony Sellers. The three of you meet for lunch, and you make the introduction.

_____

_____

_____

Situation #2

You are the purchasing agent for a large company that is in the process of buying a new and updated computer system. One of the vendors, Glenn Jones, has invited you and your boss, Jim Staff, to lunch. Make an introduction.

_____

_____

_____

Situation #3

Continuing the previous situation, Jim Staff, Glenn Jones and you are at the restaurant eating lunch. Coincidentally, your company's director of operations, Gary Moore, and Joe Head, the president, approach your table. Jim has not taken the initiative to make the introductions among his superiors and Glenn Jones. You take on the responsibility.

_____

_____

_____

Situation #4

You are attending a convention. You are talking to one of your more important *potential* clients, Steve Rich. During a lull in the conversation, a former associate with your company joins the two of you. You are in a jam because not only do you not remember the former associate's name, this woman is now working for your biggest competitor. What do you do?

_____

_____

_____

Situation #5

You have just hired Susan George to work in your accounting department. You need to introduce her to a current accounting associate, Mike Kroh. Susan and Mike will be working together as peers, both reporting to you. How should you make the introduction?

_____

_____

_____

Situation #6

You are the senior managing partner of a very prestigious law firm, which has just hired George Smiley to join the firm as an associate. All the other associate attorneys within the firm address you as Mr. Hardy. One of the partners has just introduced you as Bruce Hardy to George Smiley. What should you do?

_____

_____

_____

Situation #7

You have invited two representatives from the ABC Company, Lynn Smith, sales representative, and the marketing director, Bob Allen, to give a sales presentation at your company. In attendance are the office manager, Joe Glenn, the general manager, Judy Larny, and Brad Small, the comptroller. You are the introducer.

_____

_____

_____

Answers to Introductions Exercise

Situation #1

"John Brown, may I introduce Tony Sellers, who will be your account representative. As you know, John is one of our favorite clients from Des Moines. We specifically chose Tony to handle your account because he has many years of experience in dealing with companies such as yours. We wanted one of our most qualified people to handle your business because it is very important to us."

This example is a very touchy one because John is not yet a client; however, you have taken it upon yourself to assign the potential account to one of your subordinates. Therefore, it is necessary to establish Tony's credentials so that John feels he will benefit from the change.

Situation #2

"Jim Staff, may I introduce Glenn Jones, with whom I have been discussing the Macintosh system. Jim is our company's acquisition manager."

Jim has precedence over Glenn because he is your boss and Glenn is a vendor.

Situation #3

"Glenn Jones, may I introduce Joe Head, our company's president and Gary Moore, our director of operations. Glenn is from ABC Distributors, and we are discussing the Macintosh system."

Even though Joe and Gary have precedence over Glenn, Glenn's name is mentioned first because smaller groups have precedence over larger groups. However, Joe was introduced before Gary since he has a more important position within the company.

Situation #4

"I would like to make an introduction, and I am embarrassed to say that my mind has gone blank and I cannot recall your name." Once she gives her name (Mary Black), you say, "Mary Black, may I introduce Steve Rich with the Bowman Company. Mary and I were associated some time ago."

Note: In this particular situation, deference is being shown to Mary in order to make this encounter as social as possible, even though Steve is the "potential client" and Mary is an "associate from another company."

This is a very awkward situation. In front of a potential client you do not want to appear forgetful, which could work against you. Also, you could give your competitor an advantage. The best strategy is to admit your shortcomings in this type of situation. This can work in your favor because it shows that you are willing to acknowledge and tackle problems.

As far as giving Mary an advantage, you did not give too much information about Steve nor did you give Steve too much information about Mary. You did not divulge that Steve is considering your product or service. The only thing Mary knows about Steve is where he works, and for all Steve knows, Mary and you could have gone to school together. At this point, confine the conversation to "small talk."

A word is needed here about Mary. Chances are Mary knows you are conversing with a client or potential client, especially since you are at a convention. She was brazen to interrupt your conversation, and she should have waited until your encounter had ended to approach you.

Situation #5
"Mike Kroh, may I introduce Susan George who will be working with you in this department."

You are showing deference to Mike because he obviously has more seniority than Susan. Again, you do **not** show deference to Susan because she is a woman.

Situation #6
While greeting George, you should not say anything. However, you should take it up with the person who did the introducing once you are alone. The introducer would then have to speak to George about the proper way to address you.

Situation #7
"I have invited two representatives from the ABC Company to give us a sales presentation on a product that I believe would greatly benefit our company. Bob Allen and Lynn Smith, may I introduce Judy Larny, our general manager, Brad Small, our comptroller, and Joe Glenn, our office manager. Bob is the ABC Company's marketing director, and Lynn is his assistant."

Smaller groups have precedence over larger groups. Also, notice how deference was shown to each individual's rank within his or her group by the order in which the introduction was made.

Do not be too concerned with your mistakes. Instead, pay close attention to the reasons why you made them. If you made more mistakes than you are happy with, perhaps a review of this chapter will help.

Responding to Introductions

Knowing what to do when you are introduced to someone is just as important as being able to make introductions. You need to acknowledge the other party. This does not mean simply saying hello and walking away.

Always stand when you are being introduced. Keep your hands out of your pockets and look at the person to whom you are being introduced. Once the introduction has been made, you should greet each other by shaking hands. While you are shaking hands, there are several appropriate things to say:

- **In formal introductions,** the appropriate response is, "How do you do...," followed by the person's name. Remember always to address the person the way in which he was introduced to you.

- **In business and most social introductions,** you may say, "How are you...," followed by the person's name. In casual introductions, saying hello followed by a person's name is sufficient.

There is no need to actually answer the question, "How do you do?" or "How are you?" The appropriate response is to repeat the question, "How do you do?" or "How are you?" followed by the other person's name.

Note: This is the only instance where answering a person's question with a question is polite.

> ### *Etiquette Essential:*
>
> ***Only during introductions do you refrain from answering the question, "How are you?"***

If you run into a person you just met the day before and he asks how you are doing, you should answer his question. Be as sincere as possible but not too graphic, especially if you are not feeling well.

After the greeting has taken place, you may engage in conversation. If a savvy person made the original introductions, chances are that you know something about each other so that you can start a meaningful conversation. However, if just names were exchanged, then start the conversation by referring to your surroundings in some way.

Avoid saying things such as, "I was dying to meet you," or "I am honored to make your acquaintance." These comments put you beneath the other person. Further, save saying, "It was nice to meet you," to close the encounter.

A very uncomfortable situation arises when someone fails to introduce you. Chances are that the introducer has forgotten at least one person's name or assumes that you know the other person. At the first opportunity, initiate self-introductions. The best time is when there is a lull in the conversation.

If the introducer has made a mistake and has introduced you incorrectly, correct it right away. Simply say, "My name is...," followed by the correction. Also, if your name is difficult to pronounce, help the introducer by pronouncing it. The only situation where you should not correct a mistake is when there are titles involved, as in Situation #6 in the Introductions Exercise. Insisting on being introduced with your title makes you appear very egotistical. It is better for someone else to mention titles than claiming them yourself.

Hints for Remembering Names

Some people will help you remember their names by providing you with a cue. For instance, an unattractive salesperson named Clark, may say jokingly, "My name is Clark, just like Clark Gable." Naturally, everyone would find his analogy humorous and would chuckle with him. Rarely would anyone forget Clark's name.

However, many people have difficulty remembering names. While this can be embarrassing, it is worse to pretend that you know someone's name. Most people are intuitive enough to realize when their names have been forgotten.

If you sense that the person you are talking with has forgotten your name, refer to yourself during the conversation. Say something like, "Someone called me the other day and said, 'Elizabeth...'" You will always see relief on the other person's face when you help him out of an embarrassing predicament.

If you run into someone you have met in the past but do not recall his name, simply start by reintroducing yourself, "Hello, I'm Mary Jones. I believe we met at last year's convention." An opening such as this is an invitation for the other person to introduce himself. If the person does not take the "hint," be honest and admit that his name has escaped you and ask for it.

Etiquette Essentials:

1. **Introduce people the way they want to be known and addressed.**

2. **During introductions do *not* answer the question, "How are you?"**

4

CONVERSATION

Conversation and small talk are integral parts of conducting business. Talking to people about such things as common experiences and mutual interests builds trust and helps you forge relationships with business associates and clients.

However, many people are excellent conversationalists when the topic is business, yet feel uncomfortable if the conversation strays from their areas of expertise.

Have you ever noticed that some people appear to be bored or shy when conversation turns to small talk? More than likely, they are afraid of becoming involved in the conversation because they know nothing about the subject being discussed.

These people need to be brought into the conversation in a nonthreatening way. During a lull in the conversation, you may take it upon yourself to change the conversation by focusing on that person. Start by saying something interesting about this person, followed by a question regarding a specific interest. For instance, if this individual just opened a new business, you may say, "I would like to take this moment to congratulate Eleanor, who has just opened up her own floral shop. I know it will be successful because I have had the opportunity to see some of her work and it is unique. Eleanor, what inspires you to come up with such interesting designs?"

In this example, the focus is placed on the person in a very positive manner. Eleanor cannot fail because the subject has been changed to one that she obviously knows and likes. The other person who shines is the individual who gracefully brought Eleanor into the conversation. This example illustrates how a good conversationalist can bring a group together.

Whenever you are caught in conversation that is over your head, do not withdraw. Instead, ask questions. It is impossible to know something about everything, and these situations are opportunities to learn something new. By asking questions, you will quickly become part of the group.

Complimenting people is another good way to initiate conversations. For instance, if you are aware that someone has recently received an award (or been honored for any other type of achievement), compliment her. Keep the conversation going by asking questions about what this person has achieved.

A word of warning: Compliment people on their professional achievements as opposed to their physical qualities. While people like to hear that they look nice or that they are attractive, some do not appreciate it at all. Some compliments between members of the opposite sex may be misconstrued as "come-ons."

However, one woman telling another woman that she looks nice is a great ice breaker. For instance, "I could not help but notice how stunning you look in red." If a man said the same thing, some women would not appreciate it. Unlike most men, many women find a compliment about their looks to be more flattering when coming from another woman. However, some women find it offensive to receive compliments on their appearance from either men or women. Some older women consider it brazen when they receive a compliment from a much younger person. When in doubt, stick to compliments that involve professional or personal achievements.

A good conversationalist is often well read. Reading a wide variety of periodicals and books is an invaluable source of small talk. Scanning the local paper every day will keep you abreast of what is happening in your immediate vicinity. The two middle columns on the front page of the *Wall Street Journal* are summaries of the most important events that take place in the world, both politically and financially. Weekly news magazines such as *Time, Newsweek* or *U.S. News and World Report* are other useful sources for small talk. By reading any of these, you will be aware of global happenings in a variety of areas, such as politics, business, science, religion, the arts, etc. Due to globalization, more people are finding it necessary to become cross-culturally aware. The *National Geographic Magazine* can broaden your horizons about other cultures.

Subjects to Avoid

Every good conversationalist knows that certain subjects are taboo. The following is a list of topics that you should avoid:

- Gossip
- Your health
- Controversial social issues
- Political campaigning
- Religion
- Sex
- Profanity
- Inappropriate jokes
- Personal problems

1. Gossip

There are two types of gossip, "newsy" and "malicious." Newsy gossip may consist of the birth of a child or the announcement of someone's engagement. Malicious gossip, on the other hand, never represents people in a positive light. Do not spread or involve yourself in malicious gossip.

2. *Your Health*

Some people enjoy talking about their aches and pains, usually going into great detail about the battery of tests that they have undergone and what the doctor has prescribed. Most people do not enjoy hearing about another's poor state of health, however.

3. *Controversial Social Issues*

There are forums for discussing such controversial social issues as abortion or gays in the military, but these issues are generally inappropriate in business settings. There are already enough hurdles to overcome when doing business, so why add more obstacles to the agenda when they are not related? Avoid displaying any type of banners or wearing buttons that express your views on controversial issues.

4. *Political Campaigning*

Some for-profit organizations openly support political candidates. For the most part, however, it is not wise to overtly support any political candidate because it can unnecessarily alienate business associates or clients who may hold different views. However, being patriotic is acceptable. For instance, wearing buttons that read "I voted" or showing support for a patriotic war effort is appropriate.

5. Religion

Religion is a very private subject, and many people are sensitive to it. You may ruin an otherwise good business relationship by injecting your religious beliefs into your association.

6. Sex

Sexual harassment has become a big issue in business today. What constitutes sexual harassment is a debatable subject in itself. However, one thing is clear. If only one person finds a joke, gesture or conversation objectionable, the person who initiated it needs to stop immediately. Avoid making *any* sexual innuendos. Any discussion of sex should be avoided altogether in business.

7. Profanity

Swearing and the use of profane language have become commonplace in today's society. Nevertheless, avoid using profane or "foul" language, even if you hear such words spoken by your superiors. Once these words become part of your vocabulary, they become a habit, and habits, as a general rule, are difficult to break. One of these words may sneak out at a most inopportune time.

Some women, especially if they work in male-dominated fields, use foul language with their peers in order to gain acceptance. Avoid this pitfall. Instead, find other ways of becoming part of the team.

This is not to say that a woman should stomp out of a room in disgust when she hears foul language. In most cases, it is best to simply ignore it. After all, it is rude to point out people's faults in front of others.

8. Inappropriate Jokes

A joke does not necessarily need to be off-color to be inappropriate. Any joke that puts down a group of people falls into this category. Examples of jokes that people may find objectionable are those that make fun of a particular ethnic or religious group, people who are retarded or people who have characteristics that may be considered "different."

If someone in your group is telling these types of jokes and you or anyone else is uncomfortable with the subject matter, act accordingly. As quickly and politely as possible, change the tone of the discussion.

9. Personal Problems

Do not take your home to the office. Discussing your personal problems in business settings is generally inappropriate. The only time that a personal problem should be discussed is when it may affect your work performance, and then it should only be mentioned to your immediate supervisor. Similarly, as a supervisor, you should discuss your subordinate's problem with only those people who need to know.

Toward More Effective Speech

Your choice of vocabulary and the way you pronounce words can either enhance your level of credibility and sophistication or erode your image. However, there is a fine line between using words that can heighten your image and those that sound pretentious. The latter occurs when you try to incorporate "big" words, technical language or foreign terms when they are inappropriate for your listeners or in a given situation.

Words common to both English and another language, such as "champagne," should be pronounced with the accent common to the language you are speaking. Otherwise, it reveals a snobbish or affected attitude. On the other hand, people who mispronounce words, such as Italian with a "long i" sound as opposed to a "short i sound," reveal that they lack formal education.

Knowing the differences between the meanings of words is also important. For instance, client and customer. A "client" is a person who buys a service and a "customer" is a person who buys a product.

Some misuse of words has become so commonplace that they have become accepted as part of the English language. A good example is radio announcers who praise an athlete as "one of the best." The word "best" is misused here because there can only be one "best." It would be proper to say, "one of the better." Another word that is frequently misused is "unique." For some reason, people want to add an adjective to make something "very unique." Again, "unique" means "one of a kind;" therefore, it does not need to be "very" or "truly."

It is also important to refer to people of different ethnic groups in the way they prefer. For instance, Asians are not fond of the term "Orientals." Another common mistake is forgetting that people from South and Central American countries are also Americans, albeit, more specifically, they may be Bolivians or Brazilians.

People of Spanish descent have many different preferences. For example, some prefer to be called "Latinos," while others prefer "Hispanic." Referring to a Spaniard as a Mexican could be very insulting and vice versa. When in doubt, therefore, simply ask.

Sophisticated Words vs. Unsophisticated Verbiage

The following is a short list of examples where the first word or expression has a more decisive ring to it than its counterpart:

- All of you/you all
- Cocktail/drink
- Former/ex... (as in employee, employer or spouse)
- Good-bye/bye
- Hello/hi
- Powder room or rest room/bathroom, lavatory or latrine
- Thank you/thanks
- Very/really

5

TELEPHONE ETIQUETTE

How many times have you called a business and your call was handled so poorly that you decided to take your business elsewhere? The lesson here is: How you conduct yourself on the telephone can be as important as the impression you make in a personal encounter.

When you meet someone face-to-face, your initial impression is based on many variables. The way the person looks, how he is dressed, his eye contact, even the environment and atmosphere in which the encounter takes place are some of the factors that play a role in the impression you form of the other person. However, during a telephone conversation, the image you project is solely dependent on your words, inflection and the tone of your voice. Other considerations include background noise and how quickly the call is answered.

In this chapter you will learn some rules for using the telephone effectively in a variety of situations.

Placing Calls

Four fundamentals should be a part of any business call. They are:

1. Greeting the other person
2. Identifying yourself
3. Identifying the organization you represent
4. Asking for your party

1. Greeting the Other Person

When you place a telephone call to a place of business, always start the call with a pleasant greeting such as "hello," "good morning," "good afternoon" or "good evening."

A pleasant greeting is important because it sets the tone of the telephone call. Most people prefer to deal with people who are pleasant and friendly. Therefore, your call may go a lot further if you use an appropriate greeting.

There are times when a greeting may not be appropriate. For example, if you call a large organization where all calls go through a switchboard operator, a greeting may be inconsiderate. The telephone receptionist gets so many calls that a wordy

greeting takes time away from answering other calls
that are coming in simultaneously. In situations such
as this, be considerate and just ask to be connected to
your party or department.

2. *Identifying Yourself*

After your greeting, always identify yourself using your
first and last name or title and last name. Avoid using
your first name only or initials, such as "T.J. White,"
because it makes you sound less important. Everyone
has a first and last name, and some people hold a
professional title such as "doctor" or "reverend."
Professional titles should always be used when placing
business calls.

Some people prefer to be addressed as "Mr." or "Ms."
Typically, in business all women are "Ms." The
exception is a married woman who has taken her
husband's name. If you are attending to family matters
that include your husband, you should refer to
yourself with the title of "Mrs." However, if you are
doing business on your own, you should use the title
"Ms."

Also, use your given name when you are introducing
yourself in business situations. Given names are more
appropriate than nicknames or shortened versions of
your given name, such as "Becky" instead of
"Rebecca." Your given name will sound more
professional.

3. Identifying the Organization You Represent

Properly identifying the company or organization you represent is as important as giving your name when making a business call.

4. Asking for Your Party

Always ask to speak to a particular person rather than merely asking if he is present. Use the person's first and last name or title and last name. (For instance, "May I speak to Mark Smith?") Avoid expressions such as "Can I speak to ...?", which is grammatically incorrect; or "Is Mary Brown there?", which sounds as if you are asking if she is present, not if you may speak with her.

If the person does not hold a professional title, you may use the title of "Mr." or "Ms." This is particularly important if you are calling for the first time. In doing so, you will never be caught assuming that you may address someone without his title.

The following example illustrates the proper way to introduce yourself when making a business call.

"Good morning, I am Henry Birch with Dow Pharmaceutical Company. May I speak to Dr. Barth, please?" In this example, all the variables are there to make the formula complete.

Leaving Messages

Whenever possible, leave short messages. The message should always include your full name, the area code and number where you can be reached and a suggested time to return your call. Avoid leaving long messages. Most receptionists are not familiar with your business so the opportunity for mistakes and miscommunication is great.

Answering the Telephone

The telephone in a business office should not ring more than twice before it is answered with a pleasant greeting followed by your full name. There is no need to continue to speak after this; give the caller the opportunity to identify himself. The exception is when you are answering a line that is shared by more than one person. If this is the case, answer the call with a pleasant greeting, identify the department and then identify yourself with your full name. Consult your company's policy regarding answering calls, just to be safe.

Several years ago, the trend was to answer the telephone by simply saying your last name, "This is Smith." This is not appropriate. It sounds too abrupt, and if the caller is calling for the first time, he will not know how to address "Smith."

Answering an Associate's Telephone

Only answer an associate's telephone when you are asked to do so or if it is part of accepted office procedure. Again, answer the call with a pleasant greeting followed by the associate's name and then identify yourself. You could say something like, "Good afternoon, George Small's office, this is Gene

Smith speaking." It is important to use this format for two reasons:

1. It lets the caller know that he has reached the correct person's office.

2. It alerts the caller that he is not speaking to that particular person.

Generally, you answer an associate's telephone because he is not able to do so himself. He may be on vacation, at home sick, out of town, on a break or simply down the hall chatting with another associate. Whatever the reason, offer limited information regarding your associate's unavailability, especially if you do not recognize the caller's voice. Either say, "John is away from his desk..." or "John is away from the office..."

Emphasize your willingness to assist the caller without being too pushy or nosy. Offer the caller options, such as, "Is there anything I may do for you?" or "Would you care to leave a message?" Then it is the caller's decision which information to leave.

Answering Machines and Voice Mail

More and more companies are using automated answering systems because they are more economical and, in certain situations, more efficient. Automated answering systems are the first choice for people who spend a lot of time on the telephone or away from the office. Voice mail also allows the caller to leave longer or more personal messages without the threat that someone may misinterpret the message or hear something private.

Criticisms of automated voice systems include: they do not always work properly; they are not personal, thus sometimes causing important calls to be missed; and people do not like talking to machines. These are valid points, and in an ideal situation a receptionist or secretary initially answers the phone and also makes available to the caller the option of leaving a voice mail message.

When setting up your own automated voice system, make your announcement short. Simply say that you are unable to answer the call and ask the caller to leave a message. There is no need to apologize that you are not answering the call personally or to go into detail of your whereabouts.

Telephone Etiquette for the Receptionist

A company's receptionist is a very important person. The receptionist is usually the first contact that a potential client or customer has with a company. Therefore, the manner in which the receptionist handles the call creates either a positive or a negative impression that may remain with the caller. If the receptionist is rude or not eager to help, the caller may take his business elsewhere. If the call is handled in a pleasant and positive manner, on the other hand, the caller will feel more comfortable about doing business with the organization.

The receptionist's main job is to transfer each call to the appropriate department or person in an expedient fashion. Receptionists need to be aware of any organizational changes that take place so that they know where calls need to be transferred.

Receptionists should not chew gum, smoke or drink carbonated beverages while on phone duty. Noise from these activities can be overheard and is very annoying.

Receptionists do not need to identify themselves when answering the telephone. However, they should respond to the call with a pleasant greeting and then identify the organization.

Message Taking

When taking messages, the receptionist should note the full name of the caller, confirm the spelling of the first and last names, the telephone number, including the area code, and the time when the call was made. To avoid "telephone tag," it may also be helpful to write down a suggested time to return the call. Should the caller have a unisex name, such as "Lee" or "Pat," the receptionist should add the appropriate title of "Mr." or "Ms."

Call Waiting

Modern telephone systems are equipped with devices to let you know that another call is waiting. The most common device is a flashing light or a soft beep, which often is heard only by the party receiving the call. In either situation, the person to whom you are speaking has precedence over the call waiting. Let the person to whom you are speaking know that you have another call, ask him to hold and answer the call that is waiting. Inform the second caller that you are on another line and let him know when you will be returning the call.

Often it is necessary to take the second call before you are finished with the first caller. If you are expecting an urgent call, let the first caller know during the conversation that you may have to cut the conversation short to take the other call. If the conversation is not finished, assure the person that you will call back.

Ending Telephone Conversations

All telephone conversations should have closure; however, it should not be abrupt. Once the purpose of the telephone call has been completed, the conversation should be drawn to a close with a pleasant farewell. The appropriate farewell in business is "good-bye." It sounds more professional than "bye-bye" or "bye."

6

MEETINGS AND APPOINTMENTS

In-House Meetings

Receiving visitors in your office is similar to receiving guests in your home. Your office is your domain during working hours, just as your home is your domain during nonworking hours. Your office should represent what you do for a living and reflect a certain degree of organization. If you receive people frequently in your office, you should have a comfortable seating area to accommodate them. If long meetings are held in your office, the necessary space, furniture and equipment should be available.

When a visitor arrives, someone should escort her to your office. This could be a co-worker or secretary. Upon your guest's arrival, stand up and away from your desk, greet the visitor and show her to her seat.

If there is no one available to escort guests to your office, then go to the receiving area, greet your guest and escort her to the place where the meeting will be held. You should lead the way since you know where you are going. However, when you arrive at your office or the meeting room, allow your guest to enter first. Before sitting down, show the guest where you would like her to sit.

Remember, if you have more than one guest, be sure to observe the order of precedence when greeting and seating the visitors. Also, when receiving guests in your office, both men and women should wear their suit jackets. (This rule does not apply to women who are wearing dresses that do not have matching jackets.)

Hold all telephone calls when you are meeting, unless it is an emergency. If you are expecting a call, be sure to apprise your guest of the potential interruption before the meeting starts.

At the end of the meeting, someone needs to escort your guest to the exit. If you have a secretary to show your guest out, stand up and away from your desk and bid your guest farewell. Otherwise, escort your guest to the exit, shake hands and say "good-bye."

Chairing Large In-House Meetings

Some meetings take place in a conference room or other area outside your office simply because of the duration of the meeting or the accommodations required. In this case, you may be hosting "external clients" as well as "internal clients," and there should always be a chairperson. This person does not necessarily have to be the person who calls the meeting, although this individual may designate the chairperson.

There are many responsibilities inherent in "chairing" meetings. Depending on the formality of the meeting, certain rules should be observed. The following information pertains to the most formal sessions. Not all of it will apply to your particular situation; however, many hints may help you run more efficient meetings.

- When possible, provide the participants with an advance copy of an agenda and a roster of those who will be attending the meeting.

- If the meeting is called at the last minute, summarize the agenda at the outset and introduce the participants, if necessary.

- If the participants do not know each other, provide table tents with everyone's name; this is also a good way to strategically assign seating of attendees ahead of time.

- Equip the meeting room with adequate supplies, such as notepads and writing utensils. Niceties such as candies and beverages help create a pleasant atmosphere but are not necessary.

- Maintain a comfortable temperature in the room. Should the room become too stuffy or hot, you may suggest that the attendees remove their suit jackets.

- Start the meeting on time or determine how long to wait for those running late. If you start on time, determine whether to stop the meeting for late arrivals in order to introduce them and summarize what has been accomplished. Generally, it is better to start the meeting on time. Then, after all of the latecomers have arrived, interrupt the meeting, make the appropriate introductions and give a summary of what has been accomplished.

- Be aware of what is happening in the room by watching the participants; allow for breaks, if necessary.

- Summarize the meeting and call the meeting to a close.

Making Appointments

In some industries, guests routinely drop in unannounced. Grocery store vendors and pharmaceutical salespeople regularly call on their customers without appointments to check on how things are going or to take inventory. However, as a general rule, always make an appointment if you want to be sure you will have someone's attention. Unexpected interruptions are generally not appreciated.

When making appointments, it is a good idea to confirm them in writing, especially if the scheduled meeting is at a later date. A handwritten note confirming the day, time and location is adequate. (There is more information about handwritten correspondence in the following pages.)

If your appointment is scheduled for early in the morning, always confirm the meeting by telephone the day before. If it is to be held later in the day, you may make confirmation the same day. Appointments scheduled for Monday morning should be confirmed the previous Friday.

If you are running late, be sure to call to notify the person with whom you are meeting. Give the person the option of rescheduling or meeting you at a later time.

Upon arrival, present your business card to the receptionist and give the name of the person with whom you have an appointment. Some receptionists see so many people in a day that remembering names and companies gets confusing. By giving them your business card, you make it easier for them to announce your arrival. While you are waiting to be escorted to the meeting area, make yourself as unobtrusive as possible.

When the person you are calling on or her secretary comes out to greet you, stand up, shake hands and, if you have never met, introduce yourself. Regardless of your sex or the sex of the person greeting you, allow that individual to lead the way.

If someone other than your host escorted you, thank that person, then greet your host and allow her to show you to your seat.

Etiquette Essential:

Never take it upon yourself to choose your seat in someone's office or meeting room.

If your host doesn't indicate where you should be seated, ask where she would prefer you to sit. (**Note:** Never take it upon yourself to remove your suit coat—even if your host is not wearing one—until you are invited to do so.)

It is important to respect the person's time and not overstay your welcome. If a client or customer has limited the time of the meeting, watch the clock, and when your time has elapsed, wrap up the meeting. Chances are you will be allowed more time, but if you are not, schedule another appointment. Make an exception if the client or customer is talking or obviously carrying the conversation. In this case, be sensitive to the point at which the meeting appears to be winding down, then wrap it up.

With new clients and customers, follow up a meeting with a handwritten note thanking them for their time. Through correspondence, you show respect for the other people, and you create a positive image for yourself and the company you represent.

Participating in Large Meetings off Your Turf

If you have been invited to participate in a meeting or conference or to give a presentation outside your office, several things will help you make a good impression:

- Arrive on time. If you are running late, call and give your host an estimated time of arrival.

- Upon arriving, greet your host, mingle and introduce yourself to the other participants.

- Do not sit down until the person chairing the meeting asks the participants to take their seats.

- Arrive prepared for the meeting. If possible, get a roster of attendees with their appropriate titles and company affiliations.

- Follow the "unwritten code of behavior" regarding the removal of jackets, smoking, moving around the room, etc. Watch the other participants, in particular the meeting's leaders or senior officials, and follow their lead.

- Eagerly participate but avoid interrupting.

- Thank the chairperson for including you when the meeting concludes.

7

NONVERBAL COMMUNICATION

There are three basic ways you communicate with those around you: verbally, nonverbally and in writing. Verbal communication can either be in person or by telephone. As discussed in previous chapters, your presence on the phone and your speech in person play very important roles in the image you project.

Written correspondence is covered later in this book. However, in this chapter you will learn a second very powerful way to communicate: nonverbal communication.

Nonverbal communication consists of a person's body language, dress and other unspoken factors that combine to form an important component of one's professional image. Our perceptions of professional image are largely based on preconceived notions we either have learned from our own experiences or have been taught.

Just as advertisers create images of products, you create your own image by the way you stand, the way you dress and the way you respond to others. You "talk about yourself" unconsciously. A person who has poor posture, keeps hands, arms and legs close to the body and avoids too much eye contact is usually perceived by others as lacking self-confidence. On the other hand, people who have good posture, are relaxed and maintain good eye contact usually give the impression they like themselves.

Body Language Exercise

Imagine yourself in the following situations and jot down your reactions.

1. A person makes too much eye contact.
2. A person avoids looking you in the eye while making conversation.
3. A person glancing from your eyes to your mouth and back at your eyes while you are talking.
4. A person tapping a pencil while you are talking.
5. A woman crosses and uncrosses her legs while sitting.

6. A man sits with his ankle crossed on his knee, cradling his head with both hands, with elbows extended away from his body.
7. A woman who stands "pigeon-toed."
8. A woman who stands with her weight evenly distributed between both legs (which are spaced wide apart), with her hands buried in her pockets.
9. A person crosses his arms after a question has been asked.
10. A person crosses his arms after asking someone a question.
11. A person repeatedly rubs his chin.
12. A person sighs frequently.
13. A man looks a woman over from head to toe.
14. A woman looks a man over from head to toe.
15. A person nods his head while you are talking, but is looking at someone else in the room.

Typical Reactions to Situations Depicted in the Body Language Exercise

1. You feel "trapped" and uncomfortable, as if you are being interrogated or probed.
2. The person is hiding something from you, either the truth or himself.
3. The person is making a very sensuous gesture with his eyes.
4. The person is inconsiderate and bored.
5. The woman is either nervous or eager to leave, probably to go to the rest room.
6. The man is very relaxed. His actions are appropriate for the lounge chair at home, but too sloppy for business. His actions could also be a sign of boredom or nonchalance.

7. The woman is very feminine, almost childlike, subservient.
8. The woman is "overcompensating" with a power stance; this is very unbecoming.
9. The person does not want to answer the question.
10. The person is truly interested in what the other person has to say; he is totally focused on the other person.
11. The person is in deep thought.
12. The person is anxious.
13. The man likes what he sees.
14. The woman likes what she sees.
15. The person is not listening to a word; he wants to be elsewhere.

Should you find yourself demonstrating any of these nonverbal signals or feel people are not reacting in the way you would like, perhaps it is time to become more conscious of what your body says to others. Often, we elicit a certain response from others without understanding why.

It is also important to watch what others are doing. Often people's body language is a direct contradiction of what is coming from their mouths. A good example is Situation #15. This person may be laughing and saying, "I see." However, his focus is not on you but on the other person in the room. In this situation, close the conversation and let the person go. You will be doing yourself and the other person a favor.

Presence

Some people have the ability to draw attention to themselves by simply walking into a room. These people have "presence." People with presence draw positive attention to themselves. They are not necessarily exceptionally attractive or well dressed; however, the manner in which they carry themselves and the energy they radiate give them "presence" or "bearing."

Presence is a very powerful quality. It can be developed, and everyone should strive to attain it. However, the key to your presence lies within yourself, and only you can find it.

1. To start with, recall a time when you felt great about yourself. Where were you? Who were you with? What were you doing? What were you wearing? Had you achieved a goal? Continue to think about that time by recalling even the smallest detail, until you are actually able to experience that great feeling. Practice this exercise over and over again and pay close attention to the details so that when they are replicated, you will automatically start experiencing that feeling of greatness again.

2. Ask a friend whose opinion you respect to give you an honest evaluation of your posture and stride. Take heed of what your friend suggests and practice walking with determination and good posture.

3. Practice feeling good about yourself while you walk and stand well. Others will sense your positive energy, and it will draw attention to you. However, be careful that you do not "overly emote," because you will then be perceived as cocky, a negative quality.

Professional Dress

Dress for Success! This book title has become a slogan that is heard throughout business today. Companies hire wardrobe specialists and image consultants to work with their employees because they realize a person's outward appearance is an integral part of a company's overall image.

There are many schools of thought regarding what is considered professional and unprofessional attire. What is appropriate is totally dependent on the nature of the business and the employee's job.

Example

Three plumbers arrive to bid on fixing a broken water pipe in your office. The first arrives wearing pressed slacks, a starched shirt, open at the collar, a gold chain around his neck, cordovan loafers with matching belt, a gold watch on his left wrist and a gold bracelet on his right. You also notice that he has manicured fingernails.

The second plumber is wearing jeans with holes and his boxer shorts are poking through. Upon leaving, you notice that his shoes left stains on the carpet.

The third plumber is wearing jeans with a denim shirt, a belt and athletic shoes. He is also wearing a watch and has a pager attached to the waist of his pants.

Judging on appearance alone, who would you choose to do the work? Most people would choose the third plumber. The first plumber is overdressed for the type of work he has to do. The second plumber's appearance is sloppy, making you wonder whether his work would also be sloppy.

In this example, you can see how flashy clothes can be a negative, nonverbal clue about a person. Over-dressing can be as detrimental to your career as dressing too casually. The rule of thumb in choosing what is appropriate for your situation is to emulate the style of dress of someone within your department or profession who is respected and whom you admire. This does not mean that you should copy exactly what he wears, but try to match his style.

The Professional Look for Men

The following are general guidelines for professional men:

- Hair should be stylish and well groomed.

- Observe the "unwritten dress code" regarding facial hair. Some companies warn against beards and mustaches. Beards are usually not recommended for men.

- Fingernails should be clean and manicured.

- Cuff links are too flashy for the business day. However, they may be worn for "business after five."

- Shirts should be long-sleeved. Oxford cloth shirts are more casual than pinpoint cotton shirts. Button-down collars are more casual than straight or tabbed collars. Button-down shirts should not be worn with double-breasted jackets. Cotton shirts should be professionally laundered and pressed. Appropriate colors are white, blue, pink, yellow and ecru. Shirts may be striped.

- Ties should conform to the times. (Watch for stains, especially around the knot area, where oil from your fingers may cause discoloration.)

- Tie bars may be worn with straight-collared shirts. However, tie clasps and tie chains are not recommended.

- Suits should be stylish but not trendy. Double-breasted suits are very striking and considered to be more dressy than single-breasted suits. Appropriate colors are black, dark brown, navy blue and grey. Avoid khaki, light blue seersucker or loud plaids.

- Pocket scarves may be worn and are considered dressy. Avoid buying ties that have matching pocket scarves. But pocket scarves should coordinate with the tie.

- Belts and shoes should match in color and grain of leather. Appropriate colors are black, cordovan, dark brown and light brown. Appropriate shoe styles include laced wing-tips, laced capped-toed shoes and wing-tip styled loafers. Penny or tasseled loafers are more casual and may be worn with a sport coat and slacks. Shoes made from soft leather and soft soles are considered more casual. Patent leather shoes and boots of any variety are not recommended. Heavy western-style belt buckles are usually inappropriate.

- Socks should be the same color as the suit. Above the calf socks are recommended. (Check the condition of the heals of your socks periodically.)

- Appropriate jewelry for men is a watch, wedding band and signet ring. A tie bar may be worn with a straight collar, and cuff links may be worn after five.

- Suspenders may be worn in the business arena. However, do not wear suspenders and a belt. Suspenders should coordinate with the tie but should not be an exact match. Also, avoid wearing both a pocket scarf and suspenders.

- Handkerchiefs, umbrellas and a traditional lined trench coat are recommended.

Professional Attire for Women

The best advice to women regarding their business dress is to take advantage of their femininity in a nonsexual way. A woman should be certain that her dress calls attention to her skills and authority as opposed to her physical attributes.

- Hair should be neat-looking and in a "no-fuss" style. Long hair should be worn away from the face. Avoid wearing more than one hair ornament. A tortoise-shell or brass barrette is appropriate. Bows should be simple, preferably made from grosgrain ribbon.

- Make-up should be very discreet; less is better. Avoid colorful eye shadows (earth tones are best), too much blush and unusual lipstick colors. Wear only black or brown mascara.

- Handkerchiefs are recommended.

- A lined traditional trench coat is recommended in a neutral color.

- Nails should be well manicured and of reasonable length. "Claws" are not acceptable, nor are glittered, glow-in-the-dark or bright-colored nail polishes. Finger nail ornaments are not acceptable. Acrylic nails must be carefully maintained. Otherwise, they have a tendency to "pop off" at the most inopportune times.

- Dresses and suits should be stylish but not trendy and no shorter than directly above the knee. Very flowery patterns and certain fabrics such as brocades, satins or other shiny materials, clingy knits and voiles are not acceptable for business. Also, very feminine dresses with lace and large collars detract from a woman's professionalism.

- Medium- to small-sized handbags with shoulder straps are best suited for a professional woman because they are the least cumbersome. Women should carry their shoulder bags on the left shoulder so that they do not get in the way during handshaking. Small bags that match the shoes and are well organized are highly recommended. A woman's handbag should contain her wallet, a checkbook, handkerchief, car keys, lipstick, powder case, pen and a business card holder.

- All accessories should match. Belts, shoes and bags should be of the same color and grain. Pumps with heels not taller than two and one-half inches are appropriate. Avoid lizard or snake-skinned leathers or extravagantly styled shoes. Spectators (two-toned shoes, one of the colors being either white or bone) are appropriate in black, red, navy or brown. Black, cordovan and brown shoes are appropriate for winter. Black patent leather can be worn in the summer or winter. Taupe, bone and navy shoes may be worn year-round. Red and other bright colors are not appropriate for shoes in the business arena. Similarly, white shoes are not appropriate and should be worn only by children and brides. Shoes with sling backs or open toes and pumps with any type of ornaments are not appropriate.

- Hose should be worn in the winter. In the summer, hose were traditionally worn in the evenings or for dressier occasions. Most companies have unwritten dress codes that require women to wear hose year-round; therefore, comply when appropriate. Appropriate hose colors include taupe, natural, grey, pearl, off-black, navy and brown. Translucent hose are recommended over opaque. White and trendy colors such as green or royal blue are not recommended.

- Umbrellas are recommended.

- Jewelry should be worn sparingly. There should be a maximum of three rings, one on each ring finger and perhaps a nonobtrusive pinky ring. Avoid "cocktail" rings. One bracelet is appropriate on the nonwatch wrist. Tennis bracelets are not recommended nor are very large bracelets that make too much noise. One earring which does not dangle may be worn on each ear. One necklace, either pearls or a gold chain, is appropriate.

Some clothing and accessory taboos for a professional woman include:

- Glasses that dangle from the neck on a chain.
- Hats, except in bad weather. They should be removed before entering the office.
- White gloves.
- High boots, except in bad weather. They may be worn to the office but not in the office.
- Tennis shoes may be worn to the office but not in the office.
- Sequins on anything.
- Ankle bracelets.
- Fur coats, jackets and stoles.
- "Skorts" or culottes.
- Socks or knee socks.

More Clothing and Dress Taboos for Professional Men and Women

- **Status symbols.** These are clothes or accessories with visible brand names such as Louis Vitton, Gucci, Hermes, etc. They are considered tacky. It is best to buy things that are visually "brandless," of good quality and commensurate with what you can afford.

- **Used facial tissues.** If you are suffering from a cold, carry a package of tissues. Once they have been used, dispose of them.

- **Ill-fitting clothes**, especially clothes that are too small. If you gain weight, either have your clothes tailored to your new proportions or buy some new ones in a larger size. You will be surprised at how much slimmer you look when your clothes fit properly.

- **Unbuttoned, double-breasted coats**. Double-breasted jackets and coats should remain buttoned at all times. Single-breasted jackets and coats should remain buttoned when you are standing. They should be unbuttoned when you are seated.

- **Cologne or perfume**. Excessive use of cologne or perfume may have an overpowering effect. Some people have allergic reactions to fragrances. Use them sparingly or not at all.

- **Drastic changes in hair color**. If you decide to color your hair, seek professional help and ask that it be done over time so that it is not too shocking.

- **Wigs, hair pieces and toupees**. If you desire to wear one of these items, be certain that it is of good quality. Some have the appearance of steel wool and are very unbecoming. Again, the hair piece should be fitted professionally, and the process should be gradual so that it does not create a shock. It would be rather difficult not to display surprise if someone who is bald suddenly appeared with a new crop of hair.

Casual Attire at the Office

Many companies have designated one day a week as "casual day," because they have found that productivity is heightened when people are able to "let their hair down." Fridays and the day before a holiday starts are usually designated as casual day because they are notoriously the least productive days.

Regardless of what day it is, if you know you will be receiving guests in your office, dress professionally. Otherwise, your guests will more than likely arrive overdressed and feel uncomfortable.

The following section describes different dress code categories. Men and women should follow the dress specified under the "casual" heading on casual day. When choosing their attire for the day, both men and women need to keep in mind why casual day was brought into the business arena.

Dressing for Specific Occasions

Have you ever been invited to an evening business or social event and had no idea what to wear? Most people play it safe and wear something that would be considered neutral. Upon arrival, you would probably see people wearing a variety of clothes from casual to evening gowns and tuxedos. When you do not have the opportunity to ask what the appropriate attire is for the occasion, remember that it is better to be slightly underdressed than overdressed.

Sometimes the attire for an event is designated as
semi-formal; yet, guests arrive wearing a variety of
clothes from khaki slacks and sports jackets to cocktail
dresses and dark suits. Some hosts would be offended
if they had specifically designated the dress and still
their guests did not comply. However, many people
do not know what the different designations mean.

"Casual" could mean a variety of things. When you see
"casual" written on an invitation or the host tells you
that the dress will be casual, you need to take two
factors into consideration: the area of the country in
which the party is taking place and the socioeconomic
level of the hosts. In California, for instance, casual
could mean cut-off jeans and flip-flops. If the
invitation is from people who live in Boston, casual
may mean sports coat, tie and slacks for men and a
dress or skirt, blouse and blazer for women.
Therefore, if in doubt, ask the hosts what they will be
wearing and follow their lead. If you are hosting the
party and you know that one of your guests always
comes inappropriately dressed, you may mention what
you will be wearing for the occasion when the person
calls to R.S.V.P.

The following categories are often seen on invitations:

- Casual, business casual, country club casual
- Required country club attire
- Business after five
- Semi-formal, formal
- Formal/black tie
- Formal/white tie

Below are guidelines that will help you clarify what is meant by each category; however, if you have questions, ask your host specifically what the designation means.

Casual, Business Casual, Country Club Casual

Men: sports jacket or sweater, slacks, sports shirt (tie is optional), loafers

Women: slacks, skirts, "skorts," sports shirt, blazer or sweater, low-heeled shoes or flats

Required Country Club Attire

For both men and women, when you are invited to a private club for any type of function, whether it is golf, tennis or a meeting, first find out the dress code by simply calling the club and asking what the dress code is. Do not veer from it even slightly because you may not be allowed to participate in an activity if you do not comply with the club's dress code.

Business after Five

If you have a business function in the evening, such as a dinner meeting, awards banquet or business/social reception, there is no need to rush home and change your clothes.

Both men and women can simply "dress up" their
professional attire.

Day	**Night**
Men:	
— Dark suit	— Same suit
— White shirt	— Blue-striped shirt
— Silk tie with white symmetrical design	— White French cuffs/cuff links
	— Red tie
— Black shoes	— Same shoes
Women:	
— Off-white silk skirt	— Same skirt
— Off-white silk blouse	— Same blouse
— Fushia blazer	— Same blazer
— Bone shoes	— Same shoes
— Pearl hose	— Same hose
— Short strand of pearls	— Long strand of pearls
— Small gold earrings	— Mobé pearl earrings
	— Gold belt
	— Small evening bag
	— Cocktail ring
	— Brooch for the blazer

Semi-Formal, Formal

Men: dark suit, white dress shirt with cuff links, black shoes

Women: dressy suit or dress in silk, brocade, fine wool crepe or velvet; cocktail dress; metallic shoes; furs (if in season)

Formal/Black Tie

Men: tuxedo with black or white coats (white coats for summer only)

Women: floor-length, tea-length or short cocktail dress

Formal/White Tie

White tie is the most formal dress. Note that these categories are for the United States only. Also, white tie is traditionally not worn from June 1 through August 31.

Men: black tail coat

Women: floor-length evening gown, long gloves optional

Final Words for Image Success

When attending an affair as a couple, whether semi-formal or black tie, it is important that you are "matched." It would be inappropriate if the invitation read semi-formal and the man wore a navy blazer with grey slacks while his date wore a cocktail dress.

Even though the old adage says that "you cannot read a book by its cover," you *are* judged by the way you dress. You may be a nonconformist, but when you are at work it is important to appear as "part of the team." One of the ways you do this is by adhering to the dress code.

You should not display your individuality or eccentricity at the office or when you are invited to an event where appropriate dress is required or designated on the invitation. Out of consideration for your host, you should comply with his request. Most events have a theme, and a certain atmosphere is attained by the location, decor and type of food and drink that is served. The way in which the guests are dressed also adds to the atmosphere. For instance, if you are invited to a luau and you arrive wearing cowboy garb, you would look like a fish out of water. Your dress would be disruptive to the theme. Remember, it is as important to be a gracious guest as it is to be a gracious host.

An important note: The word "optional" when referring to dress is not appropriate on an invitation for a formal affair. Formal attire is either required, in which case it is termed "formal," or it is not required. There is no "formal attire optional" choice.

8

WRITTEN CORRESPONDENCE

Since paper was invented, people have corresponded
in writing. Today, the written word is carried by a
variety of "vehicles." In both our personal and
professional lives, we use computers, modems, fax
machines and e-mail to correspond.

No matter which method you use to communicate, the
way in which you do it will create either a positive or
a negative impression. When you receive a proposal
in writing, whether you are aware of it or not, the way
it is written and the type of stationery that is used will
contribute to your ultimate decision regarding the
message. If the proposal is written poorly and
scribbled on the company's letterhead you will look
upon it less favorably than one that arrives in an
envelope, typed and neatly presented on letterhead.

Sending personal notes to business associates can be a
very powerful tool. A note written in longhand has a
completely different impact than one that is
typewritten. A typewritten note may be a "form letter"
generated by a computer where the only difference
from one letter to the next is the address and the
salutation. On the other hand, a handwritten note on
nice stationery is perceived as much more personal.

Sending Personal Notes in Business

Send personal handwritten notes in business situations
to confirm appointments, as thank-you notes or to
acknowledge special occasions such as birthdays,
anniversaries and promotions. You may also send such
a note before a proposal or to express regrets that you
cannot attend a business or social function.

Many companies offer their employees stationery for
this purpose. It is usually greeting-card size, in the
company colors and with the company logo. Use this
only for business-related correspondence, not for
personal notes because it will make you appear
cheap.

If your company or firm does not supply
correspondence cards, then take it upon yourself to
buy some. Choose cards that are large enough for
writing a note on one side only. The best colors for
correspondence cards are white, off-white or ecru.

You may also choose a card that is similar to a
greeting card with a flap. However, this is a waste of
paper since it is customary to write only on the third

page. Instead, buy cards that are like postcards with an envelope. Your name or monogram may be embossed, thermographed or printed somewhere on the card. You may also choose to have your return address printed on the back flap of the envelope.

If possible, write handwritten notes with a fountain pen or a good ball-point pen. Never use pencil or marking pens, no matter how finely they write. The ink should be black, peacock blue or dark brown, whichever is most appropriate with the color of the stationery.

Some people like to seal their personal correspondence with wax and seal. This is an old custom that was used by the nobility when they sent their correspondence via courier. If the letter arrived with a broken seal, the recipient knew that someone had read it.

Content of the Note

If you are on a first name basis with the person to whom you are writing, you may greet her using her first name (i.e., "Dear Jane"). Otherwise, you should use the appropriate title (i.e., "Dear Ms. Jones" or "Dear Dr. Smith"). The term "Dear" is the traditional beginning of the salutation, appropriate for all sexes. It is not a term of endearment.

The appropriate complimentary closes in the business arena are:

- Sincerely
- Sincerely yours
- Respectfully
- Respectfully yours

Avoid using the following list of complimentary closes in business. They are more appropriate for personal correspondence.

- Warmly
- Cordially
- Fondly
- Yours truly
- Truly yours

If you are sending a thank-you note to a couple for an evening in which your significant other was included, it does not matter who writes the note. However, a note should be written by the person in whose business arena the evening took place. The note should be addressed to "Mr. and Mrs." The salutation should read "Dear Jane and John." The woman's name always comes first. In the body of the note, you should refer to your significant other by his or her first name, as opposed to "We would like to ..." Then it should be signed by the person who wrote the note. Do not sign for someone else.

Whenever you are mailing handwritten correspondence, always seal the envelope unless you include a card with a gift or are delivering the note yourself. In those situations, simply tuck the envelope's flap inside the envelope.

Business Correspondence

In today's business environment, executives communicate with modems, fax machines and other electronic equipment. However, the traditional business letter is still around and is not likely to be replaced.

Almost as important as the contents of a business letter is the stationery on which it is written. A company's stationery is an important part of its image. The choice of colors and style of type should reflect the nature of the business and appeal to the clientele the organization wants to reach. For instance, a law or accounting firm would want its stationery to be more conservative looking than a graphic arts company's stationery.

All business-related correspondence should be written on the company's stationery. The stationery should include the company's name, address, phone number, fax number and, if appropriate, its logo. This information should be embossed, printed or thermographed on paper that is 8 1/2 inches x 11 inches with a matching #10 envelope. Use your company's letterhead and matching envelopes for business purposes only. The correspondence should be single-spaced and either processed on a computer or manually typed, never handwritten.

All business correspondence should be neat and professional looking.

> ### *Etiquette Essential:*
>
> ### *Never send a letter with any hand deletions or corrections.*

If there are any mistakes, reprint the letter after making the appropriate corrections and adjustments.

Business Correspondence Standards

Two layout styles are used for business correspondence, block style and modified block style. In block style, all six parts of the letter start at the left margin. The text is single-spaced with an additional space between paragraphs. This style is recommended for long letters because they will appear more concise.

The modified block style is recommended for shorter business correspondence. The heading, the complimentary close and the signature start at the middle of the page. The type is single-spaced and the paragraphs are indented. Additional spacing between paragraphs is optional.

Both block and modified block styles of business correspondence are comprised of six parts:

1. Heading
2. Inside address
3. Salutation
4. Body
5. Complimentary close
6. Signature

1. The Heading

On most companies' stationery the heading is professionally printed, making it the letterhead. The heading traditionally includes the name of the company and its complete address. However, some companies elect to include other information. For example, logos, descriptions of the company's services and phone and fax numbers are common on many professionally printed letterheads.

The only part of the heading that cannot be preprinted in the letterhead is the date. For business correspondence that is written on letterhead, the date is where the heading begins. The month should be spelled out completely, followed by the numbered day of the month, a comma and then the year in numbers (i.e., 1994). Do not vary from this form, such as "1-2-94."

When sending business correspondence not related to an organization, such as a personal letter of complaint to a service company, make your own heading, including your name, complete address and the date. Your telephone number is optional.

2. Inside Address

The inside address includes the name of the person to whom you are sending the correspondence, her title, company affiliation and the company's complete address.

The name of the person should always be preceded by either a professional title, such as "Dr." or "Rev." or the appropriate courtesy title of "Mr." or "Ms." If you are using a title in the beginning of the name, avoid using any professional designations after the name, such as "D.V.M." or "Esq."

All women in business are "Ms." Only use "Mrs." when you are dealing with both husband and wife. For instance, an attorney who has written a will for a married couple should write "Mr. and Mrs. John Smith." However, if the attorney knows that the woman has retained her maiden name, the inside address would be "Ms. Jane Brown and Mr. John Smith."

A common dilemma is responding to business correspondence sent by a person whose gender is unknown to you. For instance, initials only may have been used or perhaps the person possesses a unisex name. In either case, telephone the company for whom this person works and find out if "B.J. Thompson" or "Lee Jones" is a "Mr." or "Ms."

If your first name is a unisex name, use your middle name so that your gender will be obvious. Hopefully, your middle name is not unisex as well. Never use just your initials.

The person's position should be indicated on the line below her name. Use the same title that appears on her business card. If you are unsure of the title, avoid using one or find out exactly what is correct.

A person's title is optional, but whenever possible include it out of respect for the individual's position or level of authority.

The third line of the inside address consists of the name of the company or organization that the person represents. The subsequent lines are the complete address. If your letterhead or heading uses a state abbreviation, such as "NY," you may use a state abbreviation in the inside address. However, if the state is completely spelled out in the heading, spell out the addressee's state also.

3. Salutation

The salutation is the greeting. There are two appropriate salutations for correspondence in business:

1. Dear
2. To whom it may concern

Remember that the term "Dear" is not a term of endearment but a greeting. Starting business correspondence with the person's name only, such as "Bob," makes "Bob" seem unimportant, and the entire letter may lose its professional intent.

If the person to whom you are writing does not possess a professional title and you are on a first name basis with her, you may address her by her first name. However, if you have never met or have never spoken to this person, be formal and use a courtesy title.

Use "To whom it may concern" when sending letters to an unknown person in a specific department. This salutation is gender neutral and succinct.

Salutations may be followed by either a comma or a colon; however, the comma is more professional.

4. Body of the Letter

The body of the letter includes the information that you wish to convey. Avoid using slang terms, contractions and colloquialisms.

5. Complimentary Close

All business correspondence concludes with the complimentary close. Only the first word of the complimentary close is capitalized. Appropriate complimentary closes for business include:

1. Sincerely
2. Sincerely yours
3. Respectfully
4. Respectfully submitted (when a proposal, invoice or statement is enclosed)

Complimentary closes are followed by a comma. Skip four spaces to make room for the handwritten signature.

6. Signature

The signature part of the letter is comprised of your signature with your name typed underneath. When signing business correspondence, always use your first and last name. If you have a professional designation, indicate it after your last name where your name is typed. Referring to yourself in writing as Dr. John Smith is too boastful. However, John Smith, Ph.D., is acceptable.

When signing your name, use a fountain pen or a good quality ball-point pen. The ink of the pen should be either peacock blue, black or dark brown, whichever coordinates best with the colors of the stationery.

The Business Envelope

Business correspondence is written on 8 1/2 inch x 11 inch stationery. Consequently, it requires a special envelope. Most companies have letterhead with matching envelopes. However, if you are sending business correspondence with your own heading, you need to use a business or a #10 envelope.

The return address on business correspondence is in the upper left-hand corner of the front of the envelope. The return address should include the company name and complete address only. Telephone or fax numbers are unnecessary. A logo is optional.

When you are sending a letter to a specific person, that person's name should appear on the first line of the address portion of the envelope. Again, use the professional or the appropriate courtesy title. The next line should contain the person's position in the company. Subsequent lines should include the name of the person's company and its complete address. If your return address uses a state abbreviation, you may abbreviate the state in the address portion; otherwise, spell the state out completely. The address on the envelope should be identical to the inside address.

If you are sending a letter to an unidentified person, the address portion on the envelope should start with the company name followed by the company's complete address. Then skip two lines and put "Attention: Claims Department" or whatever department is appropriate. The return address remains the same.

Invitations

Companies often hold business/social functions that involve sending printed invitations. These are similar to invitations for social occasions. Business invitations should reflect the nature of the company's business and also the type of event that will take place. Business invitations are comprised of ten parts.

1. Corporate Identification

Some companies have identifiable logos that can stand alone on written invitations. However, if you do not work for a well-known company such as MacDonald's or PepsiCo, include your company's name with the logo. The corporate identification may be placed either on the front cover of the invitation or centered at the top of a panel-styled invitation card.

2. Name of Host(s)

Business invitations must specify the name of the person or persons hosting the event. If the planned affair is to include spouses, companions or significant others, it becomes a social event. In this case, the invitation should include the spouse as one of the hosts.

Example: Use Mr. and Mrs. John Doe or Ms. Betty Smith (if her company is hosting the event) and her husband, Mr. John Smith, or Mr. John Doe and his wife, Ms. Betty Smith (if his company is hosting the event and she has retained her maiden name).

3. Invitational Statement

There are many invitational statements from which to choose. The following are recommended, beginning with the most formal:

- ...request(s) the honour of your presence...
- ...request(s) the pleasure of your company...
- ...request(s) your presence...
- ...cordially invite(s) you...
- ...invite(s) you...

In order to maintain control over the number of people you are inviting, the wording can be modified to:

- ...you and your guest... This indicates that two people may come.
- ...you are invited... and the invitation is addressed to "Mr. and Mrs. George Sales"... This means that two people may come. The invitation should be sent to the home address.

If the invitation reads, "...you and your guests...," it indicates the event is open to many guests. Call the host if you want to bring more than three people, however.

When the invitation reads, "...you are invited...," and is addressed to "Ms. Mary George," it means that just this particular person is invited.

Don't abuse the privilege of your invitation to company functions, especially if the company hosting the event is large and you happen to be their client. If you are in doubt as to how many people may come, call and find out. Remember, it is as important to be a gracious guest as it is to be a gracious host.

4. *Type of Occasion*

This part of the invitation describes the nature of the event. It will tell you what to expect: dinner, lunch, tea, etc.

5. Purpose of the Event

This part specifies why the event is being held: to honor someone, to celebrate a grand opening, to introduce a person or product, etc.

6. Date

In most invitations, the day of the month is spelled out. However, it is appropriate to use numbers when sending invitations to less formal events.

7. Time

The time of the occasion comes next. On the most formal invitation, all of the numbers are spelled out: "...at seven-thirty o'clock." You can also indicate when the party will end, "...from seven-thirty o'clock until ten o'clock."

8. Place

The place where the event will take place usually occupies at least two lines. The first line specifies the name of the actual place, such as a banquet hall or hotel. If it is not a well-known place or if you are in a large city, the second line includes the complete address. Otherwise, this line contains only the name of the city.

9. *To Whom to Reply*

This part of the invitation is, unfortunately, the most ignored. Out of consideration for the host, it is important to pay attention to this section. The party organizers need to know how many people will be attending so that they will be able to accommodate everyone. Traditionally, the wording has been "R.S.V.P.," an abbreviation of the French words for "Respond if you please" (whether you are coming or not). People receiving the invitation should respond within a week. If you have mailed an invitation requesting a response, it is appropriate to call the people on your guest list from whom you may not have heard.

It is preferable to use "Please respond by ..." with the date following the statement, rather than the traditional R.S.V.P. For some reason, people don't know what it means; they don't realize they should respond whether they are coming or not. More people heed the request to "Please respond by..." On the following line, give a phone number or the person's name to whom you wish guests to respond. This part of the invitation is located at the lower left-hand corner of the invitation and is optional.

If your company is issuing the invitations, adding "Please respond by..." will help you estimate the number of people attending.

10. Special Instructions

In the lower right-hand corner of the invitation you should place any special instructions such as "dress," "valet parking" or the need to present the invitation for admission.

If you would like to include any other information with the invitation, such as directions or a schedule of events, you may do so in two different ways. If you are using a panel invitation, simply insert another sheet with the information in the envelope. The other alternative is to use an invitation that is comprised of four pages and have the information printed on the inside cover of the card.

Forms of Address

In general, people from the United States are known to be friendly and casual. We are usually smiling, easy to talk to and have a reputation for welcoming strangers and foreigners alike with open arms. Further, we are not known to be stuffy and unapproachable. We have a tendency to be more casual than formal. These are all very fine qualities, and most foreigners will attest to the fact that Americans are helpful and down to earth. However, sometimes our casualness or lack of formality creates problems.

Some of this informality can be blamed on our language. English is one of the only major languages that does not include a "formal second person." When speaking English, regardless of whom you are addressing, the pronoun "you" is used. By comparison, most other major languages, such as Russian, French, Spanish and German, have a formal form of "you." Usually, this "you" is used between people who are business associates or new acquaintances. In some cultures, the formal "you" is even used by children when addressing their parents and between husbands and wives.

Imagine, then, a person from such a formal background meeting a U.S. businessperson for the first time. He is greeted with a slap on the back and a, "Good to meet you, Hans!" In some countries, people perform a ritual called a "Bruderschaft" where both parties cross each other's arms at the elbows while drinking a shot of vodka or some other alcohol. After this ritual both parties are able to address each other informally.

On the home front, the lack of formality may be found throughout business. Newly hired employees, fresh out of college, address their superiors by their first names, even when corporate protocol dictates otherwise. People address government officials by their first names or simply omit saying anything because they do not know how to address them.

Etiquette Essential:

If you are not certain how a person prefers to be addressed, choose the more formal approach.

If you do not know how to address somebody at all, ask for guidance. You may call the office in which this person works, or if the person is a member of the diplomatic corps, you may call the library and find out what is the appropriate address. Be aware that the manner in which you address someone verbally is usually different from the way you should address them in written correspondence.

Most Common Forms of Address

The Honorable
This is the title of choice when addressing most high-ranking American officials in office or retired, including presidential appointees, federal and state elective officials and mayors.

His/Her Excellency
This is the title of choice for a foreign high-ranking official, such as a chief of state, head of government or foreign ambassador.

Doctor (medical)
This is the title of choice for a person with an entitled degree. Use it followed by the last name when addressing the person verbally. Address a doctor in writing using his first and last name, followed by the initials of his degree; for example: Timothy Payne, D.V.M.

Academic Titles
There are two types of academic titles: doctor's degree (Ph.D.) and academic position, such as chancellor, dean or professor. When speaking to a person who holds both titles, address her with the more

distinguished academic title. An example of a verbal address is "Chancellor Davis." An example of a written address is "Dr. Richard Davis, Chancellor" or "Richard Davis, Ph.D., Chancellor of Knight University." For those without a Ph.D., use the courtesy title of "Mr." or "Ms."

Ecclesiastical Titles

All clergy have the title of "Reverend." An example of a verbal address is "Reverend Hiller." An example of a written address is "The Reverend John Hiller." You may also use the title of the position that is filled by this person in a particular denomination, such as saying, "Rabbi Goldberg," or writing, "Rabbi Israel Goldberg."

Courtesy and Other Titles

Always list degrees and professional designations in the order in which they were received: B.S., M.B.A., Ph.D.

Ms.

This is the courtesy title for all women in business. The exceptions are:

- When dealing on a professional level with a young girl who is not yet in her career path. For example, a doctor should address a 16-year-old female patient as "Miss."

- When dealing on a professional level with both husband and wife and the wife has taken her husband's last name and prefers to be addressed as such. For example, a bank officer who is opening joint accounts for a married couple should use "Mrs."

Mr.

This is the courtesy title for all men in business and when dealing with young boys not yet in their career paths.

Esquire

This is a professional designation for attorneys. However, it is not recommended to use this term after your name because it is somewhat ostentatious. This designation is not an appropriate designation for women lawyers. (Esquire is the term that was originally used for a male knight apprentice.)

Ma'am or Sir

This designation is not recommended for use in business because it makes the user sound subservient. Instead, substitute the person's name for the "ma'am" or "sir."

9

A POTPOURRI OF BUSINESS ETIQUETTE

What do you do if you are with someone who is talking your ear off and you cannot get a word in edgewise?

Is it appropriate to offer your business card to an important person you meet at a social function?

An associate has a habit that unnerves you. How do you handle the situation?

You have a cherished client and you would like to give him a gift but you do not know what would be appropriate.

Are any of these questions familiar to you? If so, read on...

"Mingling" Problems at Business/Social Functions

The purpose of many business/social functions is to create opportunities where people can expand their business contacts. Knowing how to maneuver your way through these gatherings is truly an art form, also known as "elbow rubbing."

Many organizations, especially law, accounting and engineering firms, expect their associates to be masters at "elbow rubbing" because it is good for business. However, most novices have reservations about this type of networking because they are intimidated by the prospect of approaching people.

The most common fear relates to inferiority. Many people are hesitant to approach a prospective client or customer because of that individual's perceived social status or business success.

The first thing to remember is that attending the same function puts you on equal footing with someone you may feel hesitant to approach. That is, the fact that you were included in the same social event gives you the license to talk to others who are present, no matter who they are. Simply walk up, greet them and introduce yourself.

Remember, there are only two things you need to accomplish at these functions:

1. Make a favorable impression.
2. Make a long-lasting impression.

Do not force your business card upon others but create conversation that will inspire the other person to ask about you. Hopefully, the other person will initiate an exchange of business cards. However, if that does not happen, all is not lost. Send the person a correspondence card, referring to something that was said during your conversation. At the end of your message, you may add that you would like to have the opportunity to meet with him. Then call him a week later to set up an appointment.

With any encounter, the time should be limited to a maximum of 15 minutes. Watch the other person's body language. It will let you know when you are "overstaying your welcome." If this should happen before the 15 minutes have elapsed, bring the conversation to a close *quickly* and let the other person go. Otherwise, he will avoid you at the next function.

If you are "trapped" in an encounter and the other person will not let you utter a word, avoid interrupting if possible. However, sometimes you have no choice in order to free yourself. You may say something like, "I have enjoyed hearing about your recent trip (or whatever else he was discussing), but I do need to go *now* (slightly emphasizing the word "now"). Perhaps we will be able to continue this conversation at another time. Good-bye, John." Shake his hand and leave. Next time you talk to "John," mention his trip.

Never walk away from an encounter without bringing your conversation to a close, even if there are more than two people in the group and you are not even a part of their conversation. Again, excuse yourself for interrupting and bid farewell.

If someone joins your encounter and you happen to know him, remember that it is your responsibility to make introductions. If you do not know the person and no one has made any introductions, introduce yourself.

At all business/social functions, it is wise to keep your alcoholic intake to a minimum. Hold your glass in your left hand so that your right hand will be free to shake hands. Women should have their shoulder bag hanging from their left shoulders so that it is less cumbersome when shaking hands. Carry plenty of business cards and make sure that they are in an accessible spot.

Business Cards

Business cards are very important to your professional image. The way they look and the way in which they are presented say a lot about you. A woman who must dig through her bag in order to find a business card or a man who rummages through his wallet and finally finds a card with dog-eared corners creates negative impressions. On the other hand, a person who pulls out a business card holder, opens it and offers a neat card makes a positive impression.

If you have any say in the design of the card, keep it simple. Cards that are odd sizes, cards that fold over or cards with writing on the short side are not recommended. They may be unique, but they create storage problems for those who receive them.

A business card should contain the following information:

1. Name of the company
2. Logo, if the company has one
3. Name of the card holder
4. Title of the card holder
5. Street address
6. Telephone number
7. Fax number
8. Description of what the company does, if not self-explanatory
9. Mailing address, if different from street address

Both women and men should have business card holders. The best card holders have two pockets. One side should be used for your cards and the other for those you collect. Place your cards in your holder in such a way that when you present your card the recipient will be able to read it. Never present your card facing down or sideways.

In networking situations, the exchange of business cards should be initiated by the more important person. However, if the meeting is taking place in either person's office, it should be initiated by the visitor. Business cards should not be exchanged at social affairs; it is inconsiderate of the host.

Do not include business cards in any type of business correspondence, printed or handwritten, unless you are sending company literature. In this case, you may attach your business card to the information you are sending.

Business Gifts

Everyone likes to receive gifts. However, exchanging gifts with business associates can be awkward. Some companies have strict "no-gift" policies, while others have limits on the number and value of gifts their employees may give or receive. Still others have no policy at all. Therefore, it is a good idea to check with a company's human resources department concerning its policy before bestowing a gift on one of its employees.

Gifts that reflect the nature of your business or are representative of your company are best. Also, be sure that your gift will not offend anyone's cultural background. Leather items made from cow hide would be inappropriate for some East Indians as would a timepiece for some people of Chinese origin. The following gifts should be *completely* avoided:

1. Wine or liquor
2. Meat
3. Religious items
4. Knives
5. Person items such as lingerie
6. Cash

Always keep in mind the ultimate reason for business gift-giving: to encourage more business.

Handling Difficult Situations

How do you handle a situation where someone's sense of humor is insulting or a habit is annoying? Many people feel that it is better to leave well enough alone rather than confront the individual. The key word here is "confront." Many think that discussing offensive behavior has to be a confrontation. It does not, however, if handled properly. To avoid a confrontation, use the following formula:

1. State the facts. Recall at least three different instances in which the behavior bothered you. Relate them calmly and objectively.

2. Explain the way it affected you. Recall how the problem had an impact on you and your work.

3. Offer suggestions. Suggest ways the individual can constructively and productively rectify the problem.

    If the problem elicits an emotion in you, such as crying or anger, be sure that you have this emotion in check before you confront the person.

4. If the problem has a significant influence on your work performance and it continues, **tell the person that you will be forced to take it up with someone in a supervisory position if there is no improvement and follow-through.**

10

THE MOST COMMON ETIQUETTE MISTAKES

The following list includes the most common etiquette mistakes made in business, personal and social situations. It is a quick reference that can help you avoid embarrassing situations.

Avoid...

1. Calling a business associate at home to discuss business unless it is an emergency, especially if the person is on vacation.

2. Correcting someone's grammar or pronunciation in front of others. The exception to this rule is the pronunciation of your first or last name.

3. Picking your teeth with a toothpick or flossing in public.

4. Eating directly from a buffet table without first placing the food on a napkin or plate.

5. Inviting new friends to a social event without inviting the people who introduced you.

6. Office romances.

7. Inviting someone to a social event in front of someone you are not inviting.

8. Neglecting to return phone calls.

9. Making deletions or corrections on correspondence.

10. Inviting someone to your home "for" dinner. You invite people "to" dinner.

11. Scolding subordinates or servers in front of others.

12. Complimenting people of the opposite sex on their physical attributes when in business situations.

13. Asking for an ashtray when you do not see one.

14. Neglecting to send thank-you notes.

15. Turning your drinking vessels upside down to signify that you do not want any beverage.

16. Using your napkin for reasons other than to wipe your mouth while you eat. Do not use your napkin to blow your nose or wipe the sweat off your forehead.

17. Neglecting to make introductions when you know the people present, but they do not know each other.

18. Neglecting to respond to an "R.S.V.P."

19. Pretending to be someone you are not.

20. Being a snob or looking down your nose at others.

Summary

Whenever you are confused about proper etiquette in a particular situation, measure your behavior by the following two guidelines and you will be successful:

1. Always bring out the best in the people you encounter and make them feel comfortable in your presence.

2. Think about the basics regarding precedence as it relates to age, position and group size and act accordingly.

Good luck!

Index

A

Answering machines/voice mail 48-49

B

Body language 61-64
  Body language exercise 62-64
  During introductions 19
Business cards 57, 105, 106-108
  Card holders 107
  Design 106-107
  Exchanging cards 107
  Important information 107
  Including in correspondence 107-108
Business correspondence 85-91
  Correcting mistakes 86
  Layout styles 86-87
  Six parts of business correspondence 87-91
    Body of the letter 90, 93
    Complimentary close 87, 90-91
    Heading 87
    Inside address 87, 88-89
      Titles 88-89
      Unisex names 88
    Salutation 87, 89-90
    Signature 87, 91
  Stationery 85
Business envelope 85, 91-92
  Addressing the envelope 92
  Return address 91-92
Business Notes 82-85
  Content 83-84
  Addressing the note 84
  Complimentary closes 84
  Mailing the note 84
  Salutation 83, 84
  Signature 84
Forms of address 97-101
  Addressing officials 98
  Addressing superiors 98
  Common forms of address 99-100
    Academic titles 99-100

    Doctor 99
    Ecclesiastical titles 100
    Esquire 101
    His/Her Excellency 99
    Ma'am 101
    Mr. 101
    Miss 100
    Mrs. 100
    Ms. 100
    Sir 101
    The Honorable 99
  English vs. foreign languages 97-98
Business etiquette 103-109
  Handling difficult situations 109
  "Mingling" at business/social functions 104-106
    Alcohol 106
    Business cards 106-108
    Ending a conversation 105-106
    Introductions 106
    Shaking hands 106
    Time limits 105
Business gifts 108
  Gift policies 108
  Gifts to avoid 108
Business situations 6-7

C

Clients/customers 40
Clothing
  Casual attire at the office 75
  Clothing and dress taboos 73-74
    Cologne/perfume 74
    Double-breasted coats 74
    Hair color/hair pieces 74
    Ill-fitting clothes 73-74
    Status symbols 73
    Used facial tissues 73
  Dressing for specific occasions 75-79
    Business casual 76, 77
    Business after five 76, 77
    Casual 76, 77

Conforming to the dress code 80
  Country club casual 76, 77
  Couples matching in dress 79-80
  Formal 77, 79, 80
  Formal/black tie 77, 79
  Formal/white tie 77, 79
  Required country club attire 76, 77
  Semi-formal 76, 79
  Professional dress 66-73
  For men 67-70, 73-74
    Clothes 68-70
    Hair/facial hair 67-68
    Jewelry 68-69
  For women 70-75
    Accessories 71-72
    Clothes 70-73
    Hair 70
    Jewelry 72
    Make-up 70
  Overdressing 67
  Underdressing 67
Conversations 33-41
  Compliments 34-35
  Conversations over your head 34
  Dealing with shyness or boredom 33-34
  Ethnic groups 41
  Small talk 33
  Sophisticated vs. unsophisticated words 41
  Subjects to avoid 36-39
    Controversial social issues 37
    Gossip 36
    Inappropriate jokes 39
    Personal problems 39
    Political campaigning 37
    Profanity 38-39
    Religion 38, 39
    Sex 38
    Your health 37
  Value of reading 35-36
  Vocabulary 40

D
Dignitaries 2
Diplomatic corps 2-3

E
Ethnic groups 41
Etiquette v-vii
Etiquette Essentials 5, 10, 11, 12, 19, 29, 31, 58, 86, 98
Etiquette mistakes 111-113
Etiquette Quotient Quiz vii-x

G
Greetings and farewells 9-14

I
Introductions 15-31
  Body language during introductions 19
  Couples 19, 21-22
  Forgotten names 18, 30
  Formula for proper introductions 16, 23-24
  Groups 22-24
  Introductions exercise/answers 24-28
  Pronunciations 18, 30, 119
  Remembering names 30-31
  Responding to introductions 28-30
    Business/social introductions 29
    Formal introductions 28
  Self-introductions 19, 22, 30, 31, 57
  Sophisticated introductions 18-19
  Things to avoid 20-22, 113
  Using first names 20
Invitations 92-97
  Ten parts of a business invitation 93-97
    Corporate identification 93
    Date 95
    Hosts 93
    Invitational statement 93, 94-95

Place 95
Purpose of event 95
Replying/R.S.V.P. 96, 113
Special instructions 97
Time 95
Type of occasion 94

L
Ladies vs. women debate 5-6

M
Meetings and appointments 53-59
Arriving for an appointment 57-58
Chairing meetings 54-56
Rules to follow 55-56
Following up with a handwritten
note 58
In-house meetings 53-56
Receiving visitors 53-54
Making appointments 56-59
Confirmations 57
Running late 57
Meeting off your turf 59
Guidelines 59
Time limits 58
Where to sit 58
Ms. vs. Mrs. 45

N
Names
During telephone calls 45
Pronunciations 18, 30, 111
Remembering names 30-31
Using first names 20
Nonverbal communication 61-80
Body language 61-65
Body language exercise 62-64
Handshaking 13
Presence 65-66

O
Order of precedence 1-7
Associates from competing
companies 7
Business situations 6-7

Organizational charts 6
Clients/customers 7
During meetings 54
Making introductions 16-17, 21,
23
Small and large groups 6
Establishment 3
Social situations 4-6
Older and younger people
4-5
Smaller and larger groups
4-5
Women and men 4-6

P
Protocol 3

R
Receptionists 49-50
R.S.V.P. 76, 113

S
Sexual harassment 38
Shaking hands 9-13, 57
Cold hands 12
Guidelines 10-13
Origination 9-10
Sweaty hands 12
Social situations 4-6

T
Telephone etiquette 43-51
Answering machines/voice mail
48-49
Answering the telephone 47-48
Answering for an associate 47-48
Call waiting 50-51
Ending telephone conversations
51
Leaving messages 46-47
Message taking 50
Placing calls 44-47
Asking for your party 46
Four fundamentals 44
Greetings 44-45

Identifying your organization
46
Identifying yourself 45
Receptionists 49-50
Titles
  During telephone
  conversations 45-46
  Forms of address 97-101

V
Vocabulary 40

W
Written correspondence 81-101
  Business correspondence 85-
  92
  Invitations 92-97
  Personal notes in business 82-
  83
   Correspondence cards 82-83
   Pens/ink colors 83